# Operation Z

**The quest to abolish human trafficking and rescue children who are enslaved. I am Zaysan, but this story is not about me. This book is about the kids who have been saved and the ones in the future who will be saved. Our children are indeed our future.**

# Introduction

## 502 children rescued from slavery

Do you start a war that you can not win or do you create events that will some day win the war?

I create events and save lives, one at a time, along the way…

This book is my passion to free children of the terminally poor.

This book is justice for forgotten children of the world.

This book is a message of hope that help is on the way.

This book is education and awakening.

Come walk with me, I have stories to tell.

Be brave, they need us.

We are all one after all.

The Quest will expose the bad and honor the good.

We have a plan and are making a difference.

Seek not to know the answer but to understand the question.

Join us.

# Table of Contents

# Chapter 1

## My first Experience with Child Slavery

In my line of work I feel I have used up my soul and calloused over my emotions.

I was on a little rest and relaxation from my current work as a mercenary. My last mission brought me to the region of Cambodia. I decided to stay awhile and clear my head. My usual work was negotiating ransoms for kidnappings. My team did all sorts of things for many governments around the world but most of our work was for the corporate. It all came down to one thing, liberate by any means possible. I was highly trained to adapt to any situation with what ever tools were local, including people.

The fine line between right and wrong had been walked like a tight rope.

We live a life of illusion. It is easier than knowing how things really work. We absorb ourselves in the material to escape the truth that exists with each step we take. There is a big difference between a solider for hire and a conventional solider. A solider for hire gets to choose what they do unlike a real hero that sacrifices them self under

orders of a government. We basically see the same things and do the same work but we choose which jobs to take and which ones to turn down.

But here I was, in Cambodia enjoying coffee in a little café with a great view of the people passing by in this little town I was in. I would go there every morning and sit outside by the street consumed by the noise of the motorcycles and people and trucks and so on. It was my quiet because so much was going on in my head at any given moment.

Guilt, shame, blame, anger, hate, love, forgiveness….

Like having too many voices talking at once, unable to focus on any one in particular.
So the noise from the street, the smell of gasoline, along with a good dose of pollution became my church. I could sit for hours in emptiness and tranquility.
My waiter kept me in good supply of coffee and cigars or whatever I might need. He was happy to leave me alone because he knew I always tipped well.

My work left me with paranoia.

I never knew when I would be removed from this earth by one that had escaped.

Even though I sought death, I would also fight it with all my knowledge and experience.
That is the struggle for people like me.
To wish for one thing then deny it with every particle of who you are.

The little open air café was rustic and dusty. Only a small fence definined the place where the restaurant occupied its tiny space on earth. The modest streets were mostly dirt.

Dust, debris and smoke from street venders and trash blow by as though alive. Sometimes I would sit morning 'til evening not aware of how much time had passed. Other times I would sleep all day and sit out late at night people watching. Life was taking place all around me, everyone seemed to have found a place in this world, a purpose. I would watch in wonder. What were they thinking or where were they were going? Life in these kind of places was much different from that of the USA. These people lived from day to day in hopes that life could get better but knew that was only a dream.

During the daylight it is hard to see any one pattern emerge due to the dense population. During the dark night things change drastically. It is not always a good place to be alone and not know anyone. For me however, it was actuality my comfort zone. One pattern that was now obvious was that of a foreigner milling around. It stood out like a sore thumb. I could smell the ill intention of their activity. Learning that there are tourists that seek something out in the cloak of darkness. By judging others, one defines himself. I am not like these other foreigners was my gut feeling.

These men, both white and black, paced around slowly. It was as though they were waiting for some one to approach them. Sometimes a taxi would drop them off, they would be met by a young boy. They would disappear down one of the alleys. This got my attention as it would reoccur night after night. So I decided to look a little deeper. I suspected what was going on but wanted proof. Yes I knew this would be a dangerous discovery, but knowing the truth is how I operate.

I took a walk, going the same way as those that caught my attention. If you do not know how these third world cities

are set up it is different than most could imagine. I walked up and down the many little side streets and thin alleys. Each home is different than the next. They use concrete, mud and metal. What ever they can find that will create rooms, a place to live. It is like a maze because one building can lead into another or take you into another direction. This is the kind of place that one could hide or escape very easily. One could conduct business of any kind without fear of anyone knowing. The culture here makes the impression that you don't talk or tell anyone what goes on. The people here know when and what not to talk about. The police also know this and act appropriately. Each night I delved deeper into this maze. I got to the outskirts of these shanty houses. This seemed to be the location frequented by men.

One morning, after doing this, my waiter approached me differently with my usual coffee. He inquired about my nocturnal activity. He seemed to be disgruntled with me. We had become sort of friends. I had helped get food him, along with others that worked here, and met their families. So when he saw me out at night going where the other foreigners were going he began to question who I really was. After I put his mind at ease, he was then worried for my safety. He had no knowledge of what I really did and feared I would get hurt or die in this pursuit. When I directly asked him what was going on in these places he would not answer. He just told me not to go there. He said only bad and dark, and that I would die. This is the way in many of these countries. You don't talk about things like this. You just know what everyone else knows and what you can speak of and what you don't speak of. I said I had a good idea what was going on and for him not to worry. I told him Buddha walks with me and will guide me to where I am supposed to be. This still gave him no peace.

That evening I decided to take it to the next level. It was easy to get lost as I lurked. I dressed myself as one of these men I had seen going to these outskirt shanty homes. It took no time before a boy about 12 years old approached me and grabbed me by the arm. At first I pulled away then realized I should accept this because I wanted to be like the others that came here. I did not want to give any other impression. The boy got over it quickly and asked if I wanted a girl. I told him I was just out walking. He knew I was obviously lying. What he did not know was my actual purpose in visiting this neighborhood.

I went with the boy.

I acted a bit nervous and uncomfortable which was far from the truth.

Contrastingly, it is only when my adrenaline is not pumping that I feel a sense of discomfort.

In order to remember my way out the maze of filthy hallways I scratched my arm.

This etching would allow me to count directions and find my way out.

We arrive.

He asks me what I like.

I ask him to first show me what he has.

He calls out in his language.

Words I did not understand and words I did.

The giggling of four small girls preceed their entrance to the room. They seemed genuinely excited at being chosen for me. Excited to sell themselves to me? How could this be? Were they too naïve and innocent to understand their actions?

I had to keep my emotion in check knowing what could happen if my face gave anything away.

The kindergarten aged girls were repeating one word over and over like a game, "Yum Yum".

I was not sure what that meant but could only assume.

The boy tells me they would be so happy for me to take two or three. They would be so grateful. It amazed me how this young boy could really sell. I asked how I could have sex with such a little girl. He laughed and told me, "yum yum, no boom boom". He shows me with hand gestures.

A sickness fell over me.

As tough as I thought I could be, I was weakened in the knees by the contents in my mind.

If I had been on a mission there would be no emotion and I could play any part. Here I stood in a place I had never been before. In this position I could not think of any training that would have helped me.

I knew walking in what I would see, but that still did not prepare me for this reality.

I was not in control of what was now in front of me.
I knew very well this could be a death sentence for me at
this moment.
I reached deep and thought of what if felt like to kill for the
first time.
It filled me and shifted my reality back to a place I was
comfortable with.
Not many know the feeling of facing pure evil.
Once you come face to face with pure evil you become
something else.
Some fall apart while others forget death and become what
they need to be.

I felt composed now and asked if he had anyone older. The
Boy pushed the tiny girls out and escorted seven adolescent
girls in. 12 to 14 years old was my guess. I asked boom
boom and he immediately began saying over and over
boom boom yes boom boom. I stood in front of each girl as
though I was sizing them up for a purchase. One by one
each girl looked at me with broken smiles as if they were
acting, pretending they wanted me to take them. When I got
to the last one she would not make direct eye contact with
me. I knew right away this is my target. She was the
weakest and most fearful, that would give me the greatest
ability for success.

I just discovered this place and what was going on. Had I
already decided in my mind I was here for a mission? What
was I thinking?

I started to unravel and again found myself in weakness.
The question was, am I showing it?

I looked to the boy who had backed up against the wall.
This was to allow a few older men entry to this already

crowed room. I would be expected to take one of the girls or they would get very suspicious. I knew I had to say or do something quickly. I checked my surroundings. The place was crawling with cockroaches and a few chicken bones. Then I got the idea! I got it. I jumped and kicked my feet as if trying to get something off. Everyone in the room also jumped as I went a little crazy. I began yelling the word roach again and again while moving out of the house then into street. They all started laughing and that was when I knew I had won this round. The boy was the only one to follow me to the street. I explained to him that I hate cockroaches and he bought it. He was still smiling so I told him I would be back during the day without bugs. He told me no problem and would even bring some to my hotel. With that I walked away hoping I could find my way out of this dump.

As I was walking back to my hotel I was lost over and over by what I had just witnessed. I knew what was going on but not so young. No... I did not expect that and had never really heard of that before. How?....I needed to clear my head a little so I could at least find my way to the main street. It was good I did as I noticed one of the older guys following me. This is not just a store you would visit. These people take this very seriously for ones that are not of their liking. Who knows how deep this goes? Who owns this business? The police could be involved and that would not be good for me. I walked until I was sure there was only one following, then headed to the most expensive hotel, a good distance from where I was staying. I went in and inquired about the hotel until I was sure he had lost my tail.

A boy selling cigars approached me. I bought a couple of packs and asked if he would like to make some money. Of course this is easy here, anyone will do almost anything for enough money. I had him scout for this man or anyone that

might be waiting for me. It's always good to make friends like this because they will often find you to give you updates of what is being said or what he may see. Of course he will want payment. Ahh the value of information and for 1 U.S. dollar it is worth it. Still never trusting anything.

I made my move and headed back to my place and hit the bed. All of what I had just seen now hit me. I was in a safe place where I could feel again. I got some beer and drank until I fell deep asleep.

Early the next morning, still feeling the beer from last night, I swallowed two aspirin and headed out. I found my chair by the street and got my order of coffee. I could not let go of what I had witnessed last night and it consumed me. What would I do about it? When I felt like this I knew I would not let it go and this morning sitting in my place by the street was not as great as before. I looked up to notice a foreigner taking the path I had seen so many times before, but this time it was no curiosity. It went a lot deeper and filled every fiber of my body and sickened me. I had to do something but how will this go down. I thought of how I could pull this off and actually make a difference. It seemed hopeless. As I was going through all the scenarios I began to get this feeling I always get when something is off. Someone was watching me. I began a casual scan and picked up a group of men staring at me from across the street. There were five men all about 30 years old and an older one who looked to be in his late 50's. I think they saw me looking at them and they began to move. I just ignored them so as far as they could tell and moved my chair so they had to approach from the front leaving me with an escape. I called over to my waiter and he came right away. I told him I needed another coffee and asked him who those men were. His faced dropped and he reminded me that he had warned me. Then he looked up and smiled. Then

looked back at me and said it was the priest and his body guards. Laughing he walked away to get me my coffee.

The men approached and surrounded my table just as I had wanted. They obviously did not have any proper training. The Priest sat down without an invite. He was kind of short and round and was trying to grow a beard. His glasses were large and did not fit his face as he was constantly pushing them up. His friends wore very serious faces and kind of made me laugh. I did not see any real obvious weapons and became at ease. Before the Priest could say anything I told him, thanks father for I have been looking for god and I am glad you heard these prayers. Wow, it was obvious he did not expect this. I told him to relax and tell me what he wanted with me. Then the priest looked at his friends and all seemed to relax a bit but kept their serious faces. Still on his intended speech he told me that they had seen me and knew what I was doing here. They would stop me. I ask him just what he thought I was doing here. The priest was a little taken back not knowing what was happening. So I let him in on what my belief was of why he approached me. I felt at this moment we were all caught up and relief was seen on everyone's faces.

The Priest told me about his mission to save these girls and why they approached me. He told me how many foreigners come here and the details of how they buy the girls, sometimes taking them to their hotel for days at a time. The most popular were the virgins, they made the most money off them. Once a virgin has been used they sew her up to resell her as a virgin over and over. One story after another, he was completely opening up to me. He still did not know if I was one of them he sought or if I was who I said I was.

At this moment I realized this constant pattern in me. Change. Not allowing me to get a singular focus and live a

life on one path. What the hell did I sign up for when I came to this earth anyway? Maybe it was God's cruel joke that we would laugh about once I leave this place and then when he is done with me he will send me the other direction. So, however you see it I was here to help this priest. After he told me everything, I did not ask to hear, he finally asked why I was here. So I told him a little about my life and my current talents. He was not sure how to take it, being a priest and all. It almost felt as if he was making a deal with the devil yet the deal had not been created yet. I asked him if he had a plan or if he was going to simply harass the foreigners until they went elsewhere? I know I am blunt, some may even say rude, but I find it saves a lot of time. The priest could tell that I was used to respect. He really did not know how to take me, yet no matter how many times I was direct with him, he did not shy away and leave. Then he let me in on his big plan. It was to all happen in the next few days.

They were going to raid one of the brothels and take the girls to a safe place then on to a place they could get help and education. So I ask him what was the plan and he was a little short with me. I guessed it was one of two things why this was. First he really was not sure of what he was doing or he really did not know what he was doing. So I inquire; why not ask the police for help? He went into many stories about how they were also a part of this whole mess. A couple of times they appeased him by going on raids. Every time they arrived, everyone inside had coincidentally disappeared. After a few times he realized it was not just one or two of the police that were tipping them off but the entire police force. One day he was softly approached by a Chinese man who advised him that to just leave this alone and they would do the same with him. God is not big in Cambodia. Churches are thought of more like a nuisance. He knew then that he would have to do it himself. I advised

him of the consequences and at that time he looked down. He began to explain to me how he does not understand why, but that he cannot let this go like others close to him. He realized that they will most likely be killed doing this. It is maybe one child, more or maybe none, but if he does not try what is the point of learning about all of this.

Without children there is no future. He began to cry slowly as I watched it come on. So I ask the other about their plan to raid. They had no plan. It was basically to kick in the doors with guns blazing sort of thing. I stopped them shortly after they began and told them this was their lucky day.

*******

I told them I could help with the tactical removal of the innocent, this was my experience, without exception. For the first time,  I think I had their attention. They had no real information on the lay out or number of employees and only had an idea of the number of girls. So assessing the police situation and having the guys over the next week do a lot of recon we started to have a plan. I had abducted one of the johns and got a good lay out of the brothel. I also visited the Police and had a meeting with the chief. I explained to him the cost of interfering and the ramifications to his economy.  I gave him options and waited for his response. Just as I was about to get up and leave he told me he could not let me do this. He sat with a posture of fear and at this point I knew he was worried about losing face. This is very important to their culture. I told him I understood and we each have a destiny that at one point would come together and it would be mutually beneficial for both of us. With this I knew his heart was not in this business but had outside influences that he was obligated to. I can work with this and knew we had our first step to success. So with this I returned to the hotel to wait

for one of the guys to come so we could put our information together.

Late afternoon I was beginning to wonder if we were still in progress or if the Priest got cold feet. I am sure they had someone watch me go to police. Then about 6 in the afternoon one of the guys showed and I invited him in. They had actually got a rough time schedule of the guards and number of girls. He brought to my attention that once we enter the girls would hide and we may not find them. He had done this before and found that the brothels have many hidden places and the girls may not know why we are there. This information changes a few things about our approach. I informed him what I have done and the information from the johns and would put this all together and would get back to them in a few days. He was a little set back and curious why it would take so long. He wanted to charge the place. I liked that about him but I knew the odds of doing it his way. I told him his way gives us the opportunity to get none to some and my way will get us all. I could tell he trusted me, but for me I do not like blind trust. It generally leads to the opposite effect just as fast if things go wrong. So as he was ready to leave I ask him to sit. I called office and asked them to send up some beer. We shared a cigar and drank some. I told him everything I was putting together and had him put in his input till he knew exactly what I was planning and about the conversation with the chief. I wanted him to know what I understood and maybe he could give me input about this culture. After this we were friends and I knew he would not waver and my hope was that the rest of the crew would follow his lead.

Two days later we all met to go over the plan. The little boy I hired to help me the other night was again going to be of use. I had him find me a few goons to cause a lot of trouble in town away from the brothel that would keep the attention

of all the police. Like I always say it is good to contract locals even if it is to merely buy cigarettes. We would verify the incident at the time we needed before we proceeded. It would take place when there would only be a few guards in the brothel and that is when we would hit. On the ground there was only one way in and one way out and on the roof there was little chance of escape. The ground was the best if we could find no tunnels. So it was simple: Cover all exits and barnstorm the brothel. Make a lot of noise and secure the guards. Once it was clear the Priest would enter with a couple of nuns to gather the girls. If any were missing we would locate them before we left. Some of the priests' friends would be doing watch for us out back and down the alley to a field where a windowless van would be waiting. The van would also be covered by locals that were close with the Priest. Anywhere along the way that all was not in order we had alternatives we hoped would not be necessary. One of the Priest's closest body guards was assigned to the van so we knew all would be well there. He knew what to do if he found trouble. He did not like this job because he wanted to be "in on it" but I found he was a bit too eager. Once we convinced him to cover our get away vehicle we were set to go.

We mentally and verbally drilled over and over until everyone knew exactly what we were doing.

We had many alternatives and needed to feel that all were confident and could improvise if necessary.

The most important was that all were willing to leave one of us behind if something happened and if it would jeopardize getting every girl out.

We all knew how important to save just one kid from this was worth to all of us.

I found this uncommon to have so many passionate people to accomplish this task before us.

I have heard numerous people "talk the talk", but not "walk the walk".

In this present moment I had to have confirmation and I did know.

Spirit brought all of us together for a reason, right?

*******

Early the next morning we took a trip gathering separately so not to cause attention. We drove high up on a mountain to a sanctuary for the Priests. Hidden away with a good defendable location if need be. I was surprised how willing the Priest was for me to position weapons around this place and dig holes for defense. I had a good team. This is where the calm would begin for the girls. It is where we would know if we were successful with our escape.

Once clear and calm had been realized we would begin the next step of our journey.
The girls would go further to a place where they could be with other rescued slaves.
This place I would not know until it happened. It was best for obvious reasons.
This would be where my talents would end.
Perhaps new talents would be gained.

Now we must spend a few days doing normal activities so any outside interest in us would fade.

The next morning I was in my usual place next to the little street drinking my coffee. It was not long when the priest came across the street and sat across from me with his back to the street.
I guess some of my teachings are being heard. This way I would have clear view of anyone watching with interest.  I wanted to talk to him about the mission once we got the girls out. I did not know much about the place where we would take them first, the sanctuary. Nor did I know anything about what I would call the rehabilitation center.

My talent was the tactical, not the healing of these kids.
I had to dig deep to trust the Priest knew this side of our let's say, "project".
That is the after care of  leaving the brothel.
We made sure we did not talk too loud.
The Priest enjoyed talking about this part of the plan because it was his talent.
The healing phase, not the tactile part.
That part made him very uncomfortable.
The struggle of his religion and the possibilities of taking life, along with many other sins.
It must be an extreme struggle for him.
I appreciated that.
I included this in the plan.

The Priest explained that once the kids were with us in the van,
Nuns would be in charge of communication.
All the men would remain silent and only respond when asked to.
I asked how many times has he done this and with how many at a time.
He told only a couple of times and with only a few girls.
Oh my, this is weak.
It did not give me a lot of confidence of much success.

He could see the change on my face and laughed at me.
He explained that once the kids were free with us we have already succeeded.
Where they are going is what will make the real difference.
We are nobody in this, it is the final destination that has the deepest responsibility.
That is where what they do will determine what the future will be for each of the kids.
Love is the answer and if enough is shared some will accept it.
Confused I asked what he meant by accept it.

Love was not my specialty.

The Priest saw my face again and I felt as though I must be doing something wrong.
I never give away my strength with emotions.
All of this is affecting me.
I don't know if that is a good thing or the thing that will eventually kill me finally.
The Priest explained to me that even after all we do, some girls will return to the brothels.
There are things we cannot heal.
The love for parents who sold them is something we cannot overcome.
The memories trapped in the kids minds are that which we can never understand.
We did not lose our childhood as they have.
All we can do is love them.

*******

As we continued to talk the Priest emphasized the final destination is where we win or lose with these kids. The

people there, in particular the one who runs this school, is the key. She and her staff were once one of these kids. They know how to communicate with them. The rest of us will not enter that part of the child's mind.

I asked if he would attempt conversion of religion with them.

He told me there is no one to convert in this life only to show by example.
Maybe it will be along his path and maybe another.
All we can do is help them find one.
I liked this about this priest.
He is good man who sees things similarly to me.
Show those who you are and act as you believe.
Let the universe figure the rest out.
Most important is the action.
That is what determines who we are and helps others judge us.
This all made me more comfortable about my team and my plan.
Past the brothel exit, I was at his mercy.
I was divinely guided.

I asked the Priest how he got here and how he ended up doing what he does. He told me god called him here to help the poor and starving. He was sent to spread the word of god. It did not take long for him to understand that the ones who sent him really did not know what that word was. It is great to have a picture of doing good deeds. It is quite another when you become immersed into that which presents itself all around you. Maybe he was not the best choice for their intentions of what he should be but he does not doubt his mission even one second at any time. The Priest went on and told that this is not all he does it is only one piece but it is his passion. His passion comes from his

other work. When he preaches and consults and advises he sees the hole in our souls caused by this one action, this action of selling oneself or their children to do what they feel is needed to get by just one more day. So each day whatever it is he is to do he sees all of it as a whole. It is his life not his job. I ask him where he will be when he gets old and can't do this anymore. He laughed and said my dear Z, I do not expect to get old. I could have asked for specifics to that answer, but I think he summed up the same philosophy as mine.
We will perish protecting those who can not protect themselves.

Operation Liberty, was what we were now calling our project.
What was it about these actions that I always want to give it a name?

The next couple of days went without much sleep. My mind was on repeat, seeing what could happen with this operation. Many different directions of "what if's". I seemed to do this before I went on a mission but this time I had so much Intel and time to think about it. This was not normal because usually we had to rely on our skills and abilities because the environment we were entering was mostly unknown, the end goal being our main concern. This was all new to me. I do not know if I was comfortable or the reverse. Sometimes knowing too much can cause over thinking thus slowing one down. When you act quickly on instinct and intuition, that is usually best. In the end you get the same result with the exception of time.

All would be as it was to be.
For the first time I was nervous about a mission.
That, I tell you is not a good thing.

\*\*\*\*\*\*\*

It was the morning of the mission.
Although my actions and routine followed my normal pattern,
I was in a completely different place in my mind.
My waiter had to ask me several times if I wanted more coffee.
He finally touched my shoulder and startled me.
Sure I told him, but I could tell he was about to say something.
I spoke first and comforted him by telling him I just missed home.
That satisfied him momentarily.

I told him I would be leaving in the next couple of days and then maybe finding myself missing this place too. He laughed and said he would trade with me. I could stay here and he would go to the USA. Sometimes you have to share a little white lie to protect those that you do not want harmed. He would know soon what I was really thinking about. That was ok I thought. He was a good person and would understand. He got my coffee and left me alone.

I got back to my focus. Trying to keep myself busy, I walked the streets. I occupied my mind on where I was and not what I was about to do. As I wandered the streets I thought about the yin and yang of this place. How wonderful it is with many great people but how dark it was with a very dark side. Many Places are like this, but this place caught my eye.
I was about to witness how deep and more.

I went back to my hotel for a sleep before all the activities.
The need for proper rest can not be underestimated.
My brain and body both needed this.

# Chapter 2

## The Day

I woke up feeling as if I had not slept. I never felt this
worked up by a mission before. This is no ordinary
mission. Being human is what I classify it as. Who in their
right mind would do this? I'm packed, dressed and ready to
go. I head to the lobby to pass out tips to those who have
served me well and even some that did not. Always want to
make a good and lasting impression in these sort of places.
People with less goodness in their hearts usually don't want
to be seen. The $10 I just spent goes a long way if any one
inquires about me or I want to visit here again.

I make my way out to the café. I stop long enough to drink
a quick coffee and smoke a small cigar. My timing could
not be better as I see one of my crew walking south down
the street. He is seeing me without noticing, if you
understand. He is going to see that the distraction I paid for
will actually happen. That is our signal to verify the short
staff at the brothel. At that moment we are on.

I casually make my way to the police station giving just
enough space that no one would see me. I hear a loud noise
outside and it seems as if all is going well. Like a flash my
team mate flies by and I follow. It is dark now and not
many notice us as we make our way through the maze of

structures. We spot our teammate on the roof of the brothel. He signals to us, it's a go.
Away we go!

We jump into a nearby shack that belongs to a friend of the Priest. We empty our bags, each item dedicated to this event. I check my watch. 27 seconds, not bad I thought. I had to educate my team mate on what some of the gear was. Like with any guy this stuff is uber cool. Body armor and masks, all black. At least he knew how to use his gun. I preferred long guns. We could use them as a stick, reducing the possibility of killing with them.

As we emerged from the hut we spot our teammates responsible for the positioning of rest of the team. They would not be there if there was any problem. I enter last and see one already laying on the floor unconscious with blood from his mouth. Good it was one the bad guys. I hear some yelling from another room and check one of my mates to hold his position so no one leaves. I enter the room where the yelling is coming from and see another one of my teammates holding the throat of a 15 year old boy saying something in Cambodian that did not need interpretation. He wanted to kill him and would in a matter of seconds. I understood this feeling and knew it was about to happen. I used my gun to hit the kids face sending him unconscious to the floor like a rag doll. My teammate looked at me with eyes of pure anger. I knew that look also. After a few seconds he is back in the game. We occupy the house now. No way in or out except through one of us. We go room to room but there are no girls. No noise, only heat.

The Priest breaks the rules and enters the rear of the house. I start to yell at him but it would do no good. He begins tearing up the house and opening hidden doors I had not seen. The girls flow out of the wood work. One of the trap

doors in the floor held three girls. I turn around to see one of the Priest's men come in past me with a ladder. This Priest rocks I am thinking, he knows far more than I gave him credit for. I sometimes overestimate the enemy, while underestimating my own guys.

Cleverly hidden trap doors to the attic were soon revealed.
More girls emerged.
Each smothered in sweat and panic.
The girls are confused and terrified by all that is going on.
Some even try to leave.

I witness one of our teammates weakening as girls try to pass.
I told him that this could happen.
He had to be rough like they were used to.
Force them back in.
I knew this would be uncomfortable for him.
He did not want to hurt the already wounded girls.
Alas he had to know that to save them, they may get hurt.
Then they would heal.

It was the end game that we were looking at.
We locked eyes in mental contact.
He took control by raising his voice and pushing back in our direction.

The screaming and crying sounded like the lobby entrance into hell.
In truth it was also the exit.

I climbed up the ladder to have a look inside.
It was too small and thin to imagine five girls stuffed in.
I showed my flash light around to see if any were left behind.
I see a corpse.

My stomach sank.
Wanting to retrieve it for her soul sake, I knew I could not.
She would not and that would not serve our mission.

Now 12 of the 14 were accounted for.
We knew two more were still here.

A loud bang from the next room startles us all!
I run in to see the Priest helping a kid tear apart the wall!
                                                *******

There was a hidden opening.
As the wall came off, I stood in shock.
Two girls were squeezed between the walls.
A horrible stench arose.
Even worse than before.
I was sick to my stomach.
The girls unwillingly were pulled from the wall.

Without hesitation, we all headed out the back door that
had previously been sealed to keep the girls from escaping.
We ran through the alleys keeping the girls with us, even
carrying a few of the smaller ones. Still screaming but
almost psuedo cooperating.  Maybe thinking they have new
masters.

I look at my teammates and see all the training was
working. Each watching just as I taught them to. Each
running without looking, knowing the path well, created to
be at the next phase. We stopped short of the view of the
van to verify that it had not been compromised with one in
a tree that would give us the signal to proceed. With that we
shot straight for the van and virtually threw the girls in it
with the nuns who gave us bad looks. I don't think they
appreciated our less than gentle approach. They did not

understand, but we would have plenty of time to seek their forgiveness once this part was over.

The girls calmed at the sight of the nuns, speaking directly to the women.

This was not my talent, now I was the student.

I noticed the girls did not even see the team of men anymore.
Total focus on the nuns.
Eye contact, tear filled and watery eyes.
I saw one of the smallest girls looking directly into the nun's eyes as she spoke to her.
She was intent on listening.
Shock set in on many.
Not just the girls, but for all of us.

We were fast and accurate.
Each had their part and preformed with integrity.

The Priest shocked me most with his actions.
As though he knew from the start what he would do with the ladder,
With out it being part of the plan.

As we drove over rough, wet, muddy roads the focus on watching out for anything that could spoil our trip, like followers began to fade.
Our attention began to feel the girls relax into what we had just accomplished.
This was not over for sure but the new focus was filling our thoughts.
I felt somewhat secure now.

After a long bumpy ride, we arrived.

We hid the van and let the girls out….

As we got out of the van I noticed the girls' fear of us in our gear. I see why the Priest wanted us to stay clear of the girls as we set in for the night. There would be no sleep for us as we held a continuous watch post for anything that may come our way. Constant patrols to make sure we all stayed alert.

Upon sunrise I wandered out of the compound.
I was able to appreciate the beauty of the morning light on the architecture.
I can see why the Priests come here to regain their strength in relaxation.
You do not need to know a religion to appreciate the art.
Clearly art made from those with much passion.

The Priest walked over to me. He mentioned that I had just broken the rule. The girls were not to see me until we moved on. I reminded him of the rules he broke with the ladder and we both laughed. I removed my mask as he took me in to meet the girls for the first time. Some were actually smiling now as they enjoyed a stuffed animal. They had all been bathed, hair shampooed and given new clothes. You could see peace now, in the girls and the nuns.

Over in the corner were a few of the older girls not smiling or feeling relaxed. I ask one of the nuns about this and she said they are old in comparison and carry much guilt for their life. What guilt, I asked the nun? She explained that in their culture, women are not valued. The girls are told that their families were getting money for their work. This gave them a sense of value. Now their families would no longer be sent money on their behalf.

They really don't know any other way of life because of how young they were when they began their wretched work. They don't believe they were sold. If they were abducted, why were their  parents not able to find them. They only know something has changed. Any change they have ever known has been negative. The nun said they are the hardest to save. Many end up back at the brothel. The nun assured me that where they were going would award the best opportunity to understand and get back what they lost in this part of their life. Yet it is foolish to think that they will get all of it back. I see the nun tear up and I thank her. I want to hear more, but this is not the time. Now it is the time to be strong.

I step outside the room where the girls are and stand in silence as I close my eyes. I stay close enough to hear them but out of sight. I listen to the sound coming from this room and it is almost pleasant. No more children using the vocabulary of "yum yum" or "boom boom".

I hear kids playing and adults conversing, far from the screams of hell.

*******

I think of what I would be like if I had not had this experience. What if I had looked the other way? Did I ever have a choice? Nothing I think of satisfies me. It should not be like this. I breakdown in silent tears. What is happening to me? This is not me, stop it Z!

At that moment a young nun walks in startled to see me. She pauses and smiles and looks into my eyes as I shy

away. She tells me I belong here then walks away. I compose myself and check on the guards. One by one they look at me with faces of joy. I see no tiring of focus. Who are these people now residing in my heart. This is weakness I convince myself. I am trained to be detached to be effective. Right, oh crap, now I am questioning myself. I am glad my mercenary team can't see me now. Then a familiar breath in my ear. I hear faint laughter from a deep echoing voice. As always I look around to find no one.

I walked away into the Priest approaching to gather a few of us. We were requested to remove the remainder of our gear and look ourselves. I have learned that when this priest asks of you, you do it. The Priest says he will introduce us one at a time to each girl. He will tell the girl our name. We will be escorting them to a wonderful place. They will never have to do anything they don't want to. They will be with other girls like them, go to school, cook and play games outdoors like girls should. He wanted to do it this way so that each girl would not be overwhelmed by all of us descending on them at once. One girl, one guard, all in the same room and at same time.

Each of us entered. The same short and sweet introductions were made. All of the men left the building and waited at the van. Inside the nuns explained to the girls what was happening now and how long it would take. They were told to obey the men and no one would get hurt during the transport. Told they were safe. The nuns assured them they would stay together and no matter what. Once they answered any questions the girls had (which were not many) they exited the building and entered the van. This time it was a lot different. I could see them and they could see me in a human way and not in chaos. No it was not perfect harmony but it was positive change.

\*\*\*\*\*\*\*

We were on the move again. This time I found myself
wanting to smile at them and touch their hand, but I could
not. I never felt this desire to comfort someone, to help
someone not feel afraid. My work has kept me in the
backstage, in the shadows. Those I helped never saw me or
knew me.

I am feeling vulnerable know, it is unfamiliar and making
me uncomfortable.
I have not had a lot of practice or knowledge in this part of
being human.
I am open to the possibility that it is not necessarily a bad
thing.
I am evolving again without my choice so to say.
Our drive was even longer than the night before but much
more pleasant.
The girls could relax now and share war stories in their
language.
At this moment I knew that everything was different now.
New life had been birthed.
Wonder if I can get a vacation in this new life?
Well I chose the next best thing, sleep…

In my dreams I am running away from the pain spirit drives
through my heart. There is no where to hide. Seeking love
leads to no where. I lost my light. I have lost my soul. I fear
the former actions of my life that I have been required to
serve. Am I praying? I don't know. If I am, I ask to be
released from this cycle of experience? How much can one
being take? Before I ask, the answer is already known. You
are only given as much as you can take. What did I do in
my past lives to collect so much karma? In the beginning I
accepted this path of too many directions to choose. It had

to end sometime right? When it did not, I ran. I ran towards this life of pain and sacrifice. I am to be what others needed.

Buddha appears and says to me, "Seek not to know the answer but to understand the question".

My eyes open up to see a little girl sitting next to me, innocent and sweet.
 I look to the roof of the van and out loud I say, "Fine I get it, ok"!
Shame crept in for feeling sorry for myself, I released it through a deep breath.
Finally sleep came easy.

When I woke up we were pulling into a little town that seemed to be a peaceful place, not like where we had just come from. I noticed many more smiling faces on the young girls walking around. There did not seem to be much fear here. We came to a stop and as we opened the doors I got out first since I was next to the door. I see my team also getting out.  Staying behind are the girls and nuns.  It seemed they were explaining where they were and what was happening. All the girls were intent on what was being said. Their eyes locked in with the Nuns. I jumped as a hand was placed on my shoulder. I turned to see a mature woman with glowing eyes. She looked at me directly and smiled as she brushed me aside to get to the girls in the van.

I felt absolutely no threat here and neither did anyone else. I scanned the other guys and they were all smiling. When the Priest came around he too was smiling. We have arrived at our destination! I thought to myself that my job was over and at the same time I had this feeling it was just beginning. The lady with glowing eyes motioned to follow her.  I heard the nuns calling her Mom or so I would learn

later Mam. I see other girls moving toward this area with smiles. I am finding myself not quite comfortable with all this smiling. I am really out of my element. It seems fine so I just follow. The only ones not smiling are the girls from the van and myself.

The Priest walked up to me and puts his arm around me and with his other hand grabs my hand and holds it with all smiles. "We did it, we really did it my friend," he thanked me. I watched as the girls opened up to the others like lotus blossoms blooming from the mud. Smiles emerged, the love bloom was contagious. The nuns gathered with tears of joy. Peace was in the air.

Mam walked over to me and wanted to sit. I would say that I followed her, but in truth she pulled me away. We sat in a location near the girls yet far enough away to hear each other talk. In these countries they always talk so loud and Mam was no exception. She smiled and asked why I was so stressed? She wanted me to know that I did not have to be stressed anymore. She wanted me to feel safe now. That made me smile, a little.

I asked her who she was and she told me she was these girls' mother.

When I looked around I saw a multitude of daughters, so I gathered it was her job so to speak.

The Priest already briefed her about me.
She held my hand as she told me how she had been looking forward to meeting me.
She said that I brought her many gifts…
Here many good things would happen to these girls.
She pulled me up and on to the next destination.

On our tour of the grounds she pointed out many items in need of repair.
She introduced me to many kids who were happy and sooo polite.
Along the way we stopped where some of the kids were being taught school work.
We traveled from broken pipes to walls in disrepair, broken swings to broken beds.
We saw everything from play areas to toilets.
They had it all, including vocational training.

Many other women in charge would also show me places and point out all the broken things. Who did they think I was, the handy man?
Yep! I just had to laugh.
This lady was tough and my new boss it seemed.
First I help out a priest and now I see that was my application for a handy man.
I looked around and saw I was not the only one that had been put to work.
My teammates were all working and helping with things.

She told me it cost much to raise these kids.
Since I just brought 14 this is how I would pay for some of that.
She did not ask me for money.
Still she sure was not shy about me paying her a dept.
I wondered if I would ever be allowed to leave.
Well this is the best torment I have ever been a part of.
I would flow with it.

My first priority was the thatch roof of the school.
The large straw like roof was leaking and I was trusted to repair it.
Oh this is great.
I have little experience with this and that means none.

As I improvise and wing it I am rewarded with hugs.
Everywhere I turn I witness more hugs.
Nuns hug kids, the Priest hugs Mam, teachers hug kids and kids hug kids.

As I came off the ladder to find some more materials, I was met by a little girl about seven.
She left her seat in class and asked me in perfect English, if I was repairing the roof.
I knelt down to get eye level and told her that I am trying.
She put her arms out and hugged me tight.
I was in shock and could feel myself tightening up.
I remembered what Mam told me about stress, let it go.
I was safe now.
I waited for the little girl to let go and she did not.
She said thank you and still held me.
I simply said you are welcome.

Still she did not let me go.
I was not sure what to do.
I never remember being hugged by a child.

Then she said to me, "I can't let go 'til you hug me back".
Emotion crept in on me as I felt my eyes water.
All I could think of was to hug her back.
Then she yelped like I broke her, so I let go.
She jumped and ran back to her seat laughing and everyone clapped.
The moment was over and class resumed.
It was like I was the most unaware person alive.
All I am doing is fixing a roof I thought.
By the time I collected the materials I thought I would need, the class was dismissed.

The teacher remained, looking over some papers, and asked how I was?

I said I was out of my element. She looked at me confused.
I explained I had never repaired a roof like this before and
was learning as I went.
She smiled.
What is it with all these people, do they ever stop smiling?

She noticed and knew I wanted to ask her something.  I
wondered why that little girl hugged me.  Why did she
interrupt the class, so serious that I hug her back? The
teacher told me this is not a normal school. These girls
never experienced any love that they could define. Here
they are given the opportunity to experience this where
ever they turn. You see, it is addictive to them.
She told me I looked a little awkward and disconnected.

Then she asked if I had ever been loved?

Her face turned serious and I could tell she was interested
in knowing. I looked away in thought. She knelt beside me
and touched my chin. She said we are taught to look at each
other when asked a question. My first thought was
defensive. She is not my boss. Then I looked at her and was
overcome with feeling. This seemed to be happening more
and more lately. I tried to look away again but her grip on
my chin was strong and I looked into her eyes. She told me
to answer the question. My eyes leaked.  I told her I
thought I knew love until that little girl forced a hug on me.
She laughed at me and said good boy. I told her I knew I
have been loved but it was never comfortable to return it. I
did not understand it.

People close to me in my life had all passed away.

I never felt bad for them though. I knew they really didn't
die, they just changed. I never knew where this idea came
from but knew it to be true. Maybe it was one of the things

I brought with me in this life. I had good parents and a brother. I followed everyone's lead. I had relationships but never felt completely connected. My life carried me into a war with myself. Always trying to help and serve others. On a path in a direction I could not escape. Then catching myself I stopped and wondered why I was talking so much. The teacher let go of me and smiled.

She looked as if she was thinking of what to say next. Then it came out, "Friend, you are not that different from these girls".

What, I thought? She could read my face. I am really getting bad at being a badass.

She said, "These kids never got the chance to know what is normal…Before they can learn, they are put into positions that will become their new normal. None of which they experience is real life. So being human, we absorb what is provided for us. This is our normal. These girls are taken from what they are just learning to be. Their parents are so poor. Girls have no value to them in the culture. Men are strong and can provide for family, unlike a girl. A girl only makes the family weaker, another mouth to feed. When they get a chance to sell the daughter or send them to do work in the city, then they have value. I do not think you can understand my friend because you have always had food and a place to stay, you know. Starving, not able to eat or see doctor when you are sick, puts thoughts in head that allow these things to happen. We cannot be mad at them. It is how it is. What we can do, is what we do, right here. The kids here learn in school, most others will never be in a school. They laugh and play here. Some feel like they are in a race to catch up. Once they are in environment that allows this to happen, naturally it always

does. It is our human nature to know love. The feel of real love, that's why it's addictive".

I like that word, it is the first time I have heard it used in the positive.

Now, I sit with purpose and give this teacher my absolute attention.

The teacher knows she has me now and continues with my lesson,

"You know these girls absorb their environment like it is natural because it is what humans do for survival. As we age, we carry with us what we learned from young. We being older can only relate to what we learned as a child because we are past that part of our humanity. We have other things to learn. You know other forms of survival, it is natural you know. So these kids are also our teachers too. They give us a chance to know what it is to be human".

She asked me if I understood as I looked at her speechless. She started back into her lesson again. I felt like a child in this classroom and she was my teacher. I wanted to smile but I was afraid she would do something like grab my chin again so I let her continue without any answer.
She said, "Here the children learn to read and write and do math. I think there is much more going on here and I do not need to know exactly what that is because it is right. They are all so good". Then she said she knew I had to get back to work but she had one more question for me. "My friend do you know why we all smile here"? although I had many answers in my mind, I shrugged in silence and let her tell me. She got this really big grin on her face and said to me, "You know what, we don't know either". We both

chuckled and went back to our work. I caught myself smiling from ear to ear. I whistled while I worked after that.

Ahhhhh, we must have found our selves in a vortex of harmony.

I finished up with the roof repair and headed toward the girls' dormitory.

I did not want to enter unannounced.

I saw Mam walking by so I called her over.
She came right up and hugged me.
This time I returned the hug.
She claimed I was finally letting go.
I asked her about the repairs to the housing area?
Again, it was the roof.
There was a big leak directly over one of the beds.

As I looked around I noticed not a thing out of place. The rooms were simple and colorful. Bunk beds and clean linens tell the story of this being a happy place. One of the upper bunks is covered with water from the leak so that is where I start. Then Mam teaches me what I am seeing. She taught me how sacred this room was for these girls. Where they came from this room was a place of the horror. The torment they lived in was the only place they remembered. That is why we have light hallways and open doors to all the rooms. Bright colors and love everywhere take a little while to adjust to but here is where the healing happens. They make friends. They talk at night. They know this is their home. They know this is a safe place where we do not bother them. This gives them ownership over something in their life. Before they were the property of someone else and here they find a space they can own. Not in the

material but inside themselves. So it is really important for you to fix this leak, do you understand my friend"?

I tried to give her the smile that she wears all the time but not sure if I hit the mark. I told her to stop bothering me so I can fix this for the kids. She hugged me and without a word walked out. I acquired the materials from my repair at the school so I had a good start. It did not take me as long as the school so I guess I am getting better. I took the mattress to the laundry area to be cleaned. On my way there I got lots of help to carry the mattress. A strange feeling here. Everyone helps. It is almost a game to be happy. When I arrived at laundry, they took it from me. I was then grabbed and taken by a young girl about 15 to the place they called "the shop". This is where the girls learn skills to support themselves one day.

I repaired some bolts that came loose. This happened over and over, things needing repair.
As the day passed I found myself not getting tired at all. Strangely here, I was full of energy, although I was running on empty for days.
The kitchen called us all in to eat. I did not hesitate with my sudden onset of hunger. It was amazing to watch so many people organized and happy in whatever they were doing. I did see the girls who were not smiling as they were being integrated. I walked near their sharing circle. I did not want to get too close or be a distraction so I kept a safe distance.

I did not understand the language but I did understand the sentiment due to the girls' many tears. It saddened me to see a young child so damaged and hurting. I can not imagine what was locked in their heads. I had no idea how they could heal, what I did know was this place gave them

that opportunity. It was like a hospital for humanity; who's specialty was in healing inhumane experiences.

There was nothing fake here. Everything was and is a process of healing. It was like a micro world here, an example of how to heal the macro world. I saw children with HIV and other diseases being cared for. One of the teachers told me this was a place for sick children to come die in peace. They had a place to live in the sunshine, hear birds sing and make friends until they passed. I contemplated life for a moment, the life path that we all travel down. After this experience of being with these children in this place, I am forever altered. I will never spend my time the same for the rest of my life. I am renewed.

After eating my modest meal, I walked outside to the open air in the center. I looked around and saw this place as something so special that it was hard to identify. These heinously abused children come here to overcome the shackles of their former existence. If they are terminally ill, they are given a peaceful place to pass, surrounded by love and friendship.

All the children eat, play games, and learn skills for later on. They will one day move out on their own. If they leave, they know, there is always a place to return.

I see adults with huge hearts stay here and help make all these things possible for the kids.

It is a huge sacrifice because there is no pay and really hard work both emotionally and physically. This place is so much more than the eye can see. Take me for example, I had no intention to come here to receive.

I came to deliver extra fragile packages, that no one else
could.

I was then to go on my way.
Continue my life, created for me by someone else.
But that is not really the way it turned out.
Here I learned to give back of myself and for other people.
I was healed by love too, like everyone else that comes
here.
The average eye may only see an orphanage.
To an open eye, one can see just how deeply these beings
have stepped into humanity.

# Chapter 3

## The Story of a child sex slave

Amara grew up on a beautiful country side until the age of twelve. She was often outside playing with the other kids from the neighboring farms. Things changed recently in her family of rice growers. The fields supported them somewhat fairly up until now. The government seized many farmlands for reasons never told. This caused her father to leave and find work elsewhere. He was gone for weeks at a time. One day he did not come home. It was discovered that he died in a work accident. This is not uncommon. Still never easy. The family had no money or food. Neither did the neighbors. All families there lived on a worn out thread that at any moment could break.

This was when Amara's family's thread unraveled and broke. Mother sent word to Auntie about their trouble and asked if she could help. A few weeks later, Auntie arrived with much needed food. They spent the night happy, eating then catching up in conversation. The next morning, Amara overheard them talking in a serious manor. Later Amara was told that Auntie could get her work cleaning homes in "the city".

Amara was happy to work because she wanted to help her family with all of her heart.

She felt it was her natural born duty to do so.

The Cambodian way…

Daughters are like property.

Their sole role, to provide.

The arrangements were made.

The next morning Auntie would take Amara to the city.
There would begin her domestic work.

Amara went outside to play and share her great news.
All the kids were happy for her.

It was a great day for her.

Now she could help her family.

The next day Mother was not so excited when a pick up
truck arrived as their taxi.
Amara said her good byes, but Mother seemed to show no
emotion.
Amara passed it off as Mother not able to deal with
goodbye.

The road trip was over three hours long. The truck got
stuck in the mud several times and had to be pushed out.
Along the way they stopped in other villages and picked up
more girls. It was a rough ride and all were glad to arrive in
the city. The truck stopped a few other places, one being the
police station. The driver and the police chief talked for a
while. The chief looked over the girls a few times, then
finished the conversation and went back inside. The driver
returned to driving the rickety old truck and head on down

the road. This area of the city was clean and upper class. All the girls began to dream of what it would be like to work in places like these.

Surprisingly, the truck kept right on driving.
The further they went the worse the neighborhoods got.
They were headed into the slums of Cambodia.
After they finally stopped, the mood of the driver changed to something rather dark.
He called Auntie over to him and handed her money.
Abruptly, Auntie walked away and never looked back.
Confused, Amara hollered out to her as she jumped off the back of the truck.
Men came out and stopped her as they corralled the girls like livestock.
They were pushed down a very small alley into a shack.
Amara tried looking back to see Auntie but was struck hard in the head and fell silent.

Amara woke up in a dark room by herself.

She searched for a light and the door. She found the door and hit it hard, yelling and crying.
Something crawled on her foot and up her leg. She swat it down and it fell onto other things that crawled in the dark.
Her eyes could not see a thing.

Then blinding light rushed in as the door cracked open.
The smell of a man entered.
He turned on a bare light bulb hanging overhead.
Amara's eyes instinctually shut to allow time to adjust.
At this very moment the man grabbed her arm and threw her on a small bed against the wall.
To her shock, he dropped his pants and exposed himself.
He tried to force his rooster in her mouth but she fought him.

He tried to touch her and get her to touch him, still she fought him.

When he was not successful he hit her many times.

He scolded her saying she will obey or she will die.

With that he left the room, pulling the light off as he went.

Amara sat stunned.

She felt welts on her arms and the taste of her own blood inside her mouth.

She managed to reach up and turn the humble bulb back on.

She saw bruises on her legs and felt warm blood running down her face.

Her mind was mush.

All her thoughts blurred. What did Mother do? What did Auntie do? Were they being punished too? What about the other girls? Were they being trapped in a dark place? She worried so much about what she could not understand. She looked at the room she was in. The sight of cockroaches gave the illusion that the floor was moving. Above her was a high ceiling that had a small opening in it but too tall to reach. The stained bed smelled bad like something had been butchered there. The peeling walls had once been painted pink. Posters with nude photos also clung to the walls. Next to the bed was a small night stand and on it a miniature stuffed bear.

She quickly grabbed it, hugged it and sobbed herself to sleep.

*******

Amara awoke. The door opened slowly and quietly. The light rushed in. She pushed herself back into a corner trying to escape. This time the scent of a woman entered the room, followed by her silhouette. She gently closed the door behind her. She carried a bowl of water, some rags and a candle. She approached Amara and began to clean her up.

The lady wiped her head from the dried blood and brushed her hair. She gave her a dress to put on and began to explain to her why she was here.

She was here to pay off a debt of Auntie. For this she would receive food and clothes. When the debt was paid off, she could leave. She would have to do what she was told and never try to escape. She would have to have sex with men. Amara told the lady no! She would not do this! She wanted to leave! Those were lies about Auntie. Her auntie would not put her here.

She told the woman that Mother would be worried and come looking for her.

This made the woman laugh.

She told her that her mother knew.
Auntie brought her here for this purpose.

Amara screamed and tried to get to the door. As she did another man entered and slugged her in the gut. Amara collapsed on the floor out of breath. The woman stood over her, her tone sinister now. Amara was told she would obey or be starved and beaten. If she did not submit, she would die here. The woman left the room and the man spit on Amara then kicked her as he left.

Amara could not move a muscle so she laid there for what felt like an eternity.

Days passed. She did not know how many, or what day of the week it was. She did not know or understand anything. She welcomed numbness as she lay in pain, dehydration and starvation. She never was punished before. She never acted out before or misbehaved. She never was in a place

where she knew no one. She wondered if this punishment was what was somehow best for her. Did Mother and Auntie know? She was used to being hungry but this was absolute desperation. She could not escape the sweltering heat also trapped stagnant in the room.

The door opened.
A small cup of water was placed on the floor by a young boy.

The petite boy did not look at her and scampered away quickly.

She hobbled over as slow as a sloth.

As she gulped from the cup she sounded like it was choking her.

How long had it been since she last pressed a cup of water to her lips?
How could she not remember the feeling of food against her tongue?
She lay there longing to feel full in her belly and fuller in her heart.

Soon, the little boy returned to leave a small cup of rice.
No eye contact.
Amara gobbled down half the rice before she noticed tiny bugs crawling in it.
That did not matter, she ate it without thought.
The heat finally faded.
With some food she had a little strength but will to do not much but lay there.

She could hear a commotion in the other room. Laughing and joking like people were happy. Then, a soft knock on

the door. The boy returned and entered the room and this time he looked at her. Next to him stood a mature, plump, white man with grey hair. They argued over money. The old man looked at her a few times when they were talking but never did he direct any words toward her. She did not understand his language anyway. Another man looked into the room, it was the one who had beaten her. He glared at her with evil eyes. This scared Amara to her core because all she saw was black in his eyes.

The grey man was left alone with Amara.
The door was closed.
The horny old man looked at her and smiled.

Amara trembled in fear.
She looked directly into his eyes.

He seemed to be trying to comfort her because all she could do was shake.
He touched her leg and moved up his hand.
She lacked the strength to stop it.
Her last reserve energy being consumed by tears.
As she turned away from his advances, he got angry.
He took off his clothes.
Touched her body all over.
He forcefully raped her.
Without a word, he redressed and left the room, slamming the door behind him.
She reached for the little stuffed animal and knocked it on to the bed.
There she held it in shock.

A voice, hissed like a snake in the dark.
Sssseeee, you good girl...
The door opened again, revealing the evil looking man now smiling.

He was happy to repeat himself…
Sssseee, you good girl now.
You will be fine.
He told her to get plenty of rest for tomorrow was a big day for her.

Amara could not respond or understand, only lay still in pain.
The weakness put her to sleep.
She awoke to the tender scent of noodle soup in the air.
The boy returned with her reward of noodles in hot water.
She had difficulty feeding herself.
She sipped up the water and slurped up the noodles with care.
She stayed motionless on the floor because of the pain.
She then went to the bathroom on herself because she was not able to get up.
The door opened up to the evil man and another.
They scolded her for going on her dress.
They picked her up and put her on the bed.
They lifted her dress and stitched her up her hymen.
She would be sold again as a virgin.

For the next few months the door remained locked except for the noodle soup.

Eventually, in came the new men who would "take her virginity".
Followed by the men who later sewed her back up.

When that didn't work anymore, several men were allowed in at a time.
They paid for playing out of a fantasy to "gang rape" her.

Eventually the door was left open. She did not seem to be a threat anymore.

She was too tired physically and mentally to resist.

She was dead inside. She had no thoughts.
Her brain was shutting down, like it died also.

With the door open, Amara would be called out to be seen by the customers as they arrived.
The new selection process for who would be bought.

It was like a candy store to the men. Never considering the harm on the innocent.
It was the ME society in many of the foreigners' eyes. It is what they have become.

In the eyes of the Cambodian men it was different. Once they marry, they must remain monogamous for life. So this is the common practice of the men here. It is not thought bad to have sex with young girls. In fact it is encouraged by the belief that a virgin can cleanse them of any sins or disease, including HIV.
The virgin cure all.

Amara was never permitted to leave the building.
She would have as many as 20 customers a night.
She could no longer be sold as a virgin.

Her only peace found in being able to leave her room and roam freely around the house.
She finally said hello to the other kids that lived there.

The really young ones would only do oral for obvious reasons.
The older girls talked about the men who they serviced.
It was like the childhood they started never really existed, this was the new childhood.

She learned if she pretended she wanted to be picked out of the line up,
that customer would be nicer to her and sometimes give her a tip that she would hide and keep. For what she really did not know.
Maybe some day.
Also she would earn more noodle soup than normal.
The guards would get more lax if she played the part she was supposed to.
It was survival skills at its finest.
Lately she could get close enough to the outside door that she could see the light of day.
There were shadows and noises from people moving freely about.
The outdoor air neutralized the odor inside the house.
With this new freedom she realized the large number of kids held here.
Many got sick and disappeared. No one dare ask where they went.

Not long after these new freedoms, Amara fell ill.
She would not show up for lineups.
She lay limp on that bed.
Still she was expected to service the unending customers.
One night or day, she did not know which,
A customer came in and refused her because she was so ill.

The boss came in and beat her with a wire until she bled.
He then shocked her with the same wires.
This happened more than once.
One day several men came into her room and told her she had been sold and would be leaving. As the men grabbed her she used the strength she had to grab her little stuffed animal.
Then before she was out of this place she passed out cold and lost all consciousness.

*********

She awoke in a new place.

Yet she saw the same peeling pink paint on the walls that made her feel ill.

The same provocative posters glued to the walls.

Again a hot light bulb hung from the ceiling that did not look safe to the touch.

Still in her hand was the tiny stuffed bear.

She cried herself back to sleep again.

She came in and out of consciousness.

She would wake to find adults standing next to her, only to immediately pass out again.

She did not know what they were doing to her.

Each time she would wake she would be aware a little longer.

One time she stayed awake for most of the day.

She ate again.

Each time she shared food with the bugs, it did not matter to her anymore.

When she finally washed herself, the others watched.

She was given a new dress, well new to her.

Soon after she was well, Amara returned to the line ups.

She knew what to do from experience.

Most of the girls were older than her here.

They seemed to service more of the local men, yet on occasion there would be a foreigner.

Now 10 to 15 customers a day, thus a little more freedom.

*******

All the other girls were dead inside. They seemed to have been in this life a lot longer than she. Each day she went to the front room. The guards would actually talk to her.

They liked her. Her freedom grew. Amara was becoming awake in her mind again.

She imagined escape.

As the days passed she would sit in the front room and dream about walking out the door and never coming back. She observed activities and routines of the guards. She knew when the police would arrive to get their pay off. It seemed to her that one of the police owned this house.

One day a customer came in and was very rough with her. His satisfaction was to beat her until her face became swollen and bloody. The boss thought it was her fault so the customer did not even pay. The boss crushed hot peppers on the ground and rubbed them into her wounds. When Amara became numb from this, he smeared them in her vagina. She passed out.

Once she resumed her normal routine of going into the front room, the guards no longer talked to her. In her silence, she noticed the guards left the front room unattended one day. She slowly walked to the front door and looked out. No one was there.

So she bolted.

She had no destination, hell, she had no shoes.

She ran towards the noise outside.

She ran so fast that her pains no longer hurt, she was just a shell.

Amara made it to a main street and began to look for places to hide. She thought if she could just make it to where no one would pay attention to her... Then a wack over her head made her ears ring and then everything went black.

When she came to she was back in her cage.

The door was closed. She was too weak to check if it would open.
In came the boss. He brought a jar of red ants.
They were allowed to bite her all over.
The boss stepped away pacing, yelling at her if she tries this again he would kill her.
She was not fed for a couple of days nor did she have human contact of any sort.

*******

At last they brought a pot for her to pee in and a bag to poop in.
The boy would leave some paper for her to clean it up.
She would leave it at the door to be collected.

One day the boy brought food.
Finally water came too.
The next day customers came.

The door soon was left open and she could return to freedom to move around the house. Her mind could not escape the feeling she had when she was running. It was her only good memory now. The adrenaline left her looking for the opportunity to do this again. Yet the guards watched her now so that she would never do this again.

One morning she woke up and ate her noodles then stepped into the hallway.
She heard a loud voice in her head that said one word.
RUN!
She ran straight down the hallway and out the door to the street without notice.
She ran a different direction this time.

She ran until she could not stand anymore and fell to the ground.

A woman picked her limp body up and into her house.

This woman knew what was going on and hid her.

The compassionate woman nursed Amara, fed her broth, and bathed her.

She bandaged her and clothed her, gifting her what little money she could not spare.

Amara wanted to return to Mother and Auntie.

The nice lady told her she could always come back and cried as Amara left.

******

Amara had a one track mind to find her family. She did not even notice the freedom that she had found escaping the brothel. She roamed the streets a beggar. At night she found places along the street that were hidden enough to sleep. She used her only money for much needed food. The days passed. Amara did not let on her story only that she was a relative and wanted to see her Auntie. People began to know her name and remember her.

Walking near the place people told her Auntie lived Amara looked at each house. Auntie had come up in the world. Out of her previous shack and on to her front porch. There was Auntie enjoying a refreshing beverage. Amara bellowed out to her Auntie who looked back, then away again as she entered her upgraded home. Amara ran to her door. It was locked. She pounded on the door. She yelled to open the door. Amara told the man her auntie was there and she wanted to see her. Then Amara pushed pass the man to see her auntie in the kitchen. Auntie had done well for herself with a nice house. Amara ran to her Auntie and hugged her hard. The hug was returned half heartedly. Auntie got her some water.

They began to talk. Amara asked her questions about the brothel and about being sold.
Crickets could be heard chirping,
Auntie looked at the man standing behind Amara.
She waved her hand and the man left the house.

Auntie told Amara it was all a big misunderstanding, she looked for many days to find her.

Auntie tried to change the subject many times.
Auntie fed Amara.
The man returned with another man.
This man dressed nice, but his eyes looked black.
He grabbed Amara and pulled her out the front door where other men were waiting in a car. Amara looked back and did not see Auntie.
Kicking and screaming Amara yelled into the silence,
Auntie never did appear. One of the henchmen knocked Amara out.
When she woke up she realized she was in another brothel.
She had been sold again! By Auntie!
It was all true what the others said.
Amara now accepted that her mother also knew.
At first she was sad and then angry and hurt.
She moved from place to place in her mind.
In the end she forgave both of them because this is life here.

A man entered the room and sat on the bed next to her.
He told her what was expected of her.
If she had any thoughts of leaving, she should delete them.
He told her he would cut off her arms and legs and feed her to the pigs.
With that he left.
The routine was the same but Amara was different now.

Cold and angry, she did not go to all the lineups.
She was not happy about it and the boss could tell.
One day a man came to her room and she refused him.
The boss and his men entered the room and sent the customer out.
They ripped off her clothes and laid her on her stomach on the floor.
They poked her back with a glowing hot rod.
She could smell her flesh burning each time.
She did not care anymore about the torture.
Her body was not hers anyway.
Her mind did not belong to her, it did not belong to anyone.
When it was over, the men left.
Amara laid there.
No feeling, no thinking, no anything.
The next day she saw a dress lying on the floor.
She dressed, then found food, again the bugs found it first.
Still she ate her only food.
Finally she went down the hallway into the restroom.
The door was unlocked, maybe they thought their message was heard. She could feel the burns on her back as the scars callused her emotions. She left the restroom and noticed the back door. She turned and walked in that direction. No one saw her except two girls who looked away.
Amara had the unseen powers of a zombie as she staggered out the back door and onto the street.
This time she ran because it felt good.
It was the only thing that brought her back to life.
The freedom filled her body.
She ran to any other place....
It did not matter where she was going.
All that mattered was escape and freedom.
This time she did not collapse.
She moved without fear because nothing mattered anymore. She had no family or friends, no anything. As she

walked, she smelled the street vendors cooking food for sale. Amara stopped long enough to inhale the scent……..

She was in a daze.
The person cooking could see that Amara was hungry and not a paying customer.
The street cook handed her food then shooed her away.
She attempted a smile and accepted the food as she staggered away.
She ate and felt something inside wake up.
Feeling was no longer familiar.
Visiably beaten, bruised, cut and bleeding.
Limping around without shoes.

She was a sight that did not fit the norm, even here.
She stood out, and she did not care.
She expected the worst.
She hoped for the best.
This was her life, she walked on.
While walking slowly now, she took in all the colors, sounds and smells.

Like magic, she stumbled upon a beauty salon, it really caught her eye.
She fantasized to herself what it must be like to be a customer here…
She did not notice the teenagers inside looking out at her.
They could tell who she was, with out knowing her name or story.
They too had been child sex slaves.

A small commotion arose in the salon that brought her back to the present moment.
Amara froze as the girls grabbed her arms and pulled her toward the shop.

She gave in. They got her into the salon. An older lady came out from a back room. She touched Amara's hand who was wimpering. Already knowing the answer, they asked if she just escaped. Amara could only nod yes. Amara found rescue, she was finally safe. She collapsed as all the females made a fuss over her. She did not seem to mind at all. The older lady was soft and slow in explaining what would happen next. She let Amara calm down and feel safe before she filled her with new information. When a girl was rescued, many thoughts flooded their already fearful minds. Sometimes they think the best solution is to run. There is no trust with anyone after what they have been through. Slow and steady wins the race. They ask what her name is, but she does not respond. She will talk when she is ready, one of the girls says. Amara realized she did not get hit for staying quiet.

Amara stared at a table of lunch food displayed. The girl with her sees this and asks if she would like some. Amara looks at her, afraid to get the food herself. The girl smiles and goes to the table, looking back to make sure Amara did not panic and run. This is common because of the state of mind these girls feel when they are first rescued. The girl makes a huge helping of noodles and veggies and brings it back to her. Amara inhales the food. The girl steps back a little, giving some space as to not feel like a threat. The shop owner, whom the girls affectionately call Mom, explains that she will care for the fragile girl at home where she can get clean and rest. Mom is reluctant to move her so quickly but knows there will come others looking for her. Truth is needed every step of the way. They were all afraid of her running away.

Mom addressed the fragile little bird directly, "Hello beautiful. Please eat all you want. Tell me your name so I

don't have to call you girl". This time Amara spoke her name softly.

Mom said it was a nice name, meaning everlasting beauty... With that Amara shed a little smile.

Amara decided not to fear this lady. Mom came close to touch her hand but Amara pulled away. Mom understood. She looked at Amara and asked to gain her trust her now. Mom understood what she endured because she was once long ago in her position of torment. She gave the other girls job training here so one day they could do this job. The girls could leave anytime they want and go anywhere they want, but not without telling Mom. She was their Shepherd, they her beloved lambs. If she yelled at them it was only because was protective and loved them as her own.

It was explained that people were probably looking for her, she believed it to be true. Amara said nothing and really did not need to. Mom told her that she could stay as long as she wanted to, but to be safe they needed to get to a house as soon as possible. At the shop there was no protection and a confrontation was possible. A friend with a car would come, but Mom was concerned that Amara may fear being returned back to the brothel. Mom did not know that Amara had escaped once to her auntie, only to be resold. However, Mom is pretty well educated when it comes to these stories. She did not want anyone to see Amara, but also didn't want her to fear recapture. She asked if Amara would agree to get into the car. With that Amara broke into tears. Mom hugged her and for the first time Amara did not pull away from touch.

Walking was an option, if they had help. She looked at Amara's sweet and devastated face and could tell from her

eyes this would be the best way to travel. Mom stood up, she knew she would need about five other women to help create a hive around her.

She thought about closing the salon but that would only draw suspicion. She paced the room and called in her troops. The other women were not given details, simply told to come assist as soon as possible. She told Amara that help was on the way and all would be good. Mom instructed one of the girls to fetch a change of clothes so no one would suspect anything. With that the girl smiled and waved at Amara then was off to her task.

Mom was on a new mission which was slightly comical to watch. Mom was moving around the shop in a frenzy. Amara almost cracked a smile at Mom's actions. Amara had a bit of trust in her and this could go a long way. Mom sat down to share her plan. They would walk in a group to a safe house where she could relax. Mom's friends would stay to see if anyone else came looking. Then all the women would join up…. There was nothing to fear, these women were really good people. She wanted Amara to get to know them, it is never a bad thing to make friends around here. Her eyes started to tear up she told Amara to trust her because she will help her to never worry about this again. As mom started to cry, Amara reached up and wiped her tears then hugged her. They sat there hugging until one of the ladies arrived.

As the other ladies arrived it got louder with each one. Each one acknowledged Amara. Then the girl arrived with the clothes so Amara could go and change. She started to close the door on her so she could have privacy but stopped and left the door open a little so Amara would not be afraid. While Amara changed the ladies gathered and Mom explained with as little detail as necessary. All of them seemed to understand fully and did not question Mom.

They would have a good time on their walk and not draw much attention so to get to Moms house.

Many do not know that when there is a force of women like this it is a good thing to stay away unless you want to join in. Men see this and never pay any attention because they are afraid of women in a group. They are only brave when a woman is alone. So the women kept the emotion in a positive place. Everyone knew the plan. Mom went to Amara and told her it was time and made sure Amara was fine with it. She told Amara if she saw anyone she knew to grab moms arm or hand and she would take care of it. Amara looked in Mom's eyes and knew they were ready.

Out the door they went, walking, talking and looking at all the little shops. Amara was not really watching the ladies, she only stared at all she was seeing. This was the first time she had been in the city in a way she could look at things. Mom kept her close. She did not allow her to stray. Amara was in a zone that was as if she was a fly on the wall, a spectator. Not feeling a connection to anything, observing only. She did not really pay attention to the direction they were headed, if anything went awry, she would be lost.

They made it to the house and went inside. Amara was first with Mom right behind. The other ladies continued shopping to see if anyone was around. Amara stood looking around at this little home not rich by any means but not at the poverty level either. Mom had her sit down on a chair and offered her a soda. Amara never had a soda before and just looked at Mom. Amara sipped the fizzy drink. A huge smile grew across her face that made everyone laugh. All the ladies were in the house now and so it became quite chatty. Amara observed the laughter. This is so different than anything she had experienced. She relaxed in a chair among the noisy yet comforting feminine energy.

Eventually she closed her heavy eyelids and fell into a deep sleep, perhaps the deepest in the last two years.

# Chapter 4

## After the Escape

Amara had a few days of being spoiled which she did not
mind at all. Still she remained empty, there was something
missing in her. It was an emptiness that she could not
explain. Amara's journey started with loving family and
friends. Day by day experiences. Being betrayed by her
family after her father's death was pure hell. She finally
escaped from the only thing she could remember, the
brothel...It was the longest two years of her life. Now she
could accumulate new experiences. Shape who to become
and let go of the memories of the past...Voids and holes
manifest as we grow, life finds those experiences that are of
use and weeds out the others. For youth like Amara who
are taken from their natural habitat is like rebooting a
computer with a different program. Starting over each day
to find value to fill the void...Happiness is necessary to
make a child's life whole. No matter how much love, Mom
can give to Amara it is beyond her knowledge to help
Amara fill this void. Now that Amara has found a sense of
calm Mom knew she must take her to a place that can do
the most good. Help relieve the shame, guilt and loss of
innocence.

This would not be an easy conversation with Amara. This
wouldn't be easy for Mom to let go of this beauty of a child
whom she has taken in. Mom did realize all though she got
her to safety she could not take her to the next level needed
in her life now. So she made breakfast and told Amara that

it was time they had a talk. Amara really was open to anything Mom said now. Amara was learning trust so anything that came her way now will be questioned by her soul. Mom explained to Amara that she needed help from people like her that were better educated on this life's lesson. Mom explained about her story and how she found rescue. She had not until now told Amara her story, only that she too had been a child sex slave. Amara sat and listened with intent and full attention. Amara knew she had a deeper connection with Mom than she understood. She was the first person to give off a feeling of guarded safety over her like an angel. Amara will never trust anyone again. She would know when it felt right…Amara was much stronger than most girls in her situation. Still she had fear and doubt that would last a century.

Mom told her that tomorrow she would take her to a better place that can do much more for her…. She also told Amara that she did not have to stay and could come home with her. Mom explained that if she could she would keep her forever and protect her and take care of her but she knew that Amara really needed what this place could offer her. If Amara agrees they would make this trip and she could decide. Amara asked questions about this place. Where is it? Who are the people? What would she do there? The questions came out like bullets in a machine gun, one after another. Mom laughed and told her to calm down. It was obvious that all this was sinking in on Amara. Mom told her they are kind people that grew up like she did and now have helped many other girls like her. They know and understand what you are feeling when you feel it. They take care of your health with food every day. You will not be a queen, you too will have to help with the chores my dear. It is a safe place where you will not have to worry about any of the bad people finding you. You will learn to play again and maybe even trust people. There is a school

where you can learn all you will need to know when you decide it is time to leave. Yes, you will decide when to leave. Amara lit up when she heard she could go to school. There were so many thoughts swirling in her head she almost felt dizzy.

Mom could tell this was overwhelming to Amara and reached over and hugged her. "My girl you can always come visit me. I hope you will always be in my life. Maybe you come to work for me doing hair and nails, I am sure my girls will love that. They always want more of an army to go against my rules. Amara laughed a little and that was a very good sign to Mom. There are many things you will learn and I know there will be times when you feel sad and lonely but I want you to remember that there are others that will feel the same as you. Some will be sick and about to die from the diseases that come with this life. You may be the strength to help them. After what I went through, what really kept me going was not to allow the sadness to overtake me. If I felt that happening I would help someone else. It's an evil that will take you if you let it. If you become your boss then you will have nothing to fear you amazing little girl! You are so brave to escape and that tells me you have hope. You may not know you did so I wanted to tell you.

What I learned to survive is that we need three basic things in our soul:
1-      We have to have love for our selves.
2-      We need hope. Without hope we have no purpose.
3-      We need trust. Without trust we are and will always be alone.

*******

The next morning Mom was emotional getting ready to make the trip. Amara could see this so she silently crept up and hugged her. Mom had some tears and this time Amara did not. Maybe her emotions had callused over, but Mom did not seem to mind. Mom saw the strength in Amara and it helped her collect herself. Outside one of the ladies arrived in a motorcycle taxi. She smiled and told Amara that the driver was her son and could be trusted. Amara looked at him closely and gave him the stare. The young man simply smiled and motioned for them to come... The motorcycle included a glamorized sidecar that is used everywhere in Asia. It had a roof and window and space for several Asians to sit but not so much for foreigners if you get the picture. Today it would only be Mom, Amara, and her friend. Mom held Amara tight and told her to watch, incase she ever needed to remember. They rode about forty five minutes 'til they were out of town. Off the road a little were some brick structures and grass huts. Amara started to get a little nervous and Mom picked up on it. She asked the driver to stop, he did. It seemed everyone knew this would happen. They were about 40 meters from the entrance gate. The place had a small wall surrounding it. Amara looked and could see many girls her age and younger walking around. Some stood near the gate. She also noticed some older ladies walking around taking care of things. One woman stood out from the other because she was smiling ear to ear and waving.......

Everyone was elated to see them arrive! The smiling woman hugged them all then turned her focus to Amara…She bent down a little to be eye to eye with her. They all welcomed her in.     She was told that she would get to go to school, have her own bed, get to make friends and have fun. Everyone called the smiling woman Joan and she seemed to be well liked among all the other girls.

Joan offered to show them all around and explain the rules. Amara looked at Mom with a worried look. Mom smiled back and told her everything was okay.

They all walked at Amara's pace so she could soak in her surroundings. The beautiful property was sprawling with grass, trees and a small pond. What really caught her attention were several girls sitting in a circle under a roof with no walls. They looked very serious and one was crying. The other girls were being attentive to her. There was an older woman sitting in the circle, talking to her softly. She could not hear what was being said but it seemed caring and compassionate. Amara learned that every girl who comes here must talk about all that has happed to them. That is part of the healing process here. Letting the truth set them free. Joan explained that if you want to be soft you must first know hard, and if you want to be hard you must first know soft. Here they were taught how to no longer identify as victims. She was told that she could have the satisfaction of life with out fear or loneliness, but she would have to give this place a chance. .......

They walked a little further into the center and came up to the kitchen. Most of the people preparing lunch were girls like her. A loud woman who was over seeing it all, waved and invited them to stay for some food. The woman joked and said she didn't know if it would taste good but they could stay and decide for them selves. With that everyone broke out in laughter…This put Amara at ease. Ah the good medicine of old fashioned laughter and food made with love.

They all sat and Joan served them the food… She told Amara not to get used to this service and next time maybe she could serve her. They all laughed and started to eat. It was very simple food, rice and some greens. With clean

drinking water, everyone seemed content... Amara looked around at the girls eating and smiling. All appeared well and this made her feel at ease in her environment.

After they finished their meal Joan told Amara to gather all the bowls and follow her. They walked to the sinks and washed together before they continued with their tour. Joan playfully splashed Amara with some of the soapy water. Amara was beginning to let down some of her walls, even if just a teeny tiny bit..... When going back to the table Amara carried a towel with her. Joan asked why and Amara playfully joked that it was for Joan to finish wiping down the table. Joan stopped and smiled to herself because she knew Amara had spirit... So many of the girls don't have this and end up back in the brothels. No matter how much is done for the girls it is ultimately up to them.

Next they walked to the bedrooms. As they approached Amara noticed no doors and plenty of light from the open windows. She heard laughter and chatter from the girls in there squealing. Joan scolded the girls to go outside if they were going to make so much noise. The girls laughed and ran outside, showing no fear. Amara was relieved to see all this and know that Joan was not as mean as she thought. So Joan showed her the rooms where the girls slept. It had two bunk beds with mosquito nets pulled open. Each girl had a small stand on the floor level and the upper bunks had a shelf with little objects of theirs. It was real Amara thought as she gazed at the hello kitty stuffed animal on one of the clean and tidy beds...Mom touched Amara on the head and guided her outside to see what else they could find out in the courtyard....

Next they head to the school, no walls, just a roof. A soft spoken male teacher wrote the lesson on a blackboard. When they got closer everyone looked at Joan and her

group. One of the younger girls got up and ran over to Joan and hugged her. The girl was about 6 years old. Joan smiled and yelled at her to get back to her class. The little girl smiled and went back to her seat as instructed. Amara shyly asked how to find the restroom. Mom pointed her in the right direction and she went. All though there was no door it was still private, nothing fancy but very clean. Once finished she went back to the group where they walked on to a large garden area.                 Joan motioned to the back where some girls were picking vegetables. Joan took them back to see some of the food that was grown here. It was limited due to lack of funds but it was still special. She said some of the girls enjoyed gardening and reminded Amara that everyone joins together to get all the jobs done.

Amara spotted some boulders and asked if they could sit on them. They were big enough for all to sit on and talk next to the tranquility of the pond. Amara was curious if there were fish in the water. Joan said maybe, but that no one knows how to catch them to find out. Amara thought back to her father, alive, fishing with her. Maybe she could teach the others how to do it. Joan smiled and told Amara that would really be nice. Amara was opening up to the idea of staying for a while. Joan reminded her that she would not be mistreated here but she would have to stay in line and obey the adults in charge. Joan was a kind boss and it showed.

She explained how she worried that the girls would get upset and leave if the rules were too strict, "You know my little flower, sometimes I think that you girls sit in your room and talk about how mean I am. At first I get scared a little and wonder if I am always correct in the things I do. You know we all make mistakes. What I know is if I make a mistake it is not because I am trying to be bad but because I love you girls. I will never ever harm you and I

know my people here will never harm you. So Amara I need you to trust me on this. It can be difficult here, but if you believe me, you will soon see. Mom and I exchanged telephone numbers. You can call her anytime. There is only one phone here so it is not always free, but it is yours to use. Please know that at times you will have to wait, OK"? She agreed and smiled at both the women.

Joan continued, "Mom is giving me some money every month to help pay for you. I want you to know this and appreciate it because it is difficult here to afford all these girls and most don't have anyone that cares so much for them outside of here. I promise I will take care of you and keep you safe. So my girl you want to see your bed"? With that, Amara was showered in hugs and kisses from Mom who was now crying. As they parted Amara stopped and ran back to Mom and hugged her. She told Mom she would be ok and not to worry for her. Then they broke apart and Amara rejoined Joan.

Amara was given a nice bottom bunk bed with a few drawers underneath for her future belongings. "This is your space, you can keep it how you like, as long as you remember that you will be sharing the room with three other girls. You will all get along. In the morning I want you to go over to the place where you saw all the other girls sitting in a circle, do you remember"?
Amara told her yes and asked how she would know the time to go. Joan reassured her that the other girls would wake her. She was told that breakfast was served before daily activities. She was also told that her teacher was a Nun, who would find her and invite her to class. Amara and Joan sat down on her bed for a heart to heart chat. They seemed to understand each other. With tears in their eyes they embraced. Amara was home.

They really connected. This does not happen often in this place because of all the painful memories shared. Each person deals with it differently. More often than not these children never open and heal. Some have the desire but lack the environment to do so. Even in the best rescue centers there is still 40% loss rate. The girls can't find the peace they lost a long time ago and return to the brothel or someplace worse. Yes there are places that are worse than the brothels. That is another story for another time. On the other side of this are the ones who survive and heal the wounds. They find their strength through embracing their truth. Many go on to become happy and successful people. Some will even go on to marry and have families, but most can't handle that part of their womanhood. Some become Joan's themselves. They see a purpose and a passion to hold out their hands and lift another like them up. It is not a job but a calling.

Amara and Joan sat there holding each other before Joan got up and returned to her work. Amara was curious to know what her work would be here. Joan told her do not worry because she can explore until that is determined. Her main responsibility would be attending the daily meetings. Amara was reassured that she was aloud to have fun and with that Joan left the room. She sat alone in the room for a moment and almost thought back to that first time that she was left alone in a room, but instead decided to run outside into the sunshine. She ran like a torpedo towards the other girls and actually knocked one of them down.

Amara got scared. The other girls laughed. They helped her up and asked where she was going in such a hurry. She had no answer. The tallest girl asked if she was okay as she brushed the dust of her clothes. The girls asked if she was to be their new roommate, so Amara pointed to her room and they smiled. They told her they would have fun but

they had to be quiet at night because Joan will come screaming at them. With that mental image they all laughed, including Amara.

The taller one introduced herself as Thien and Amara returned the introduction. The other girls ran inside the building where the rooms were. Thien told Amara that they were all going down to the pond to play. She invited Amara to go with them. Amara did not answer because she was not sure what she was supposed to do. Thien noticed the hesitation,    grabbed her arm, pulling her along the path. Amara did not resist. They got about half way and heard a thundering behind them, it was the other girls running to catch up. Thien saw this and laughed with Amara. Finally Amara made a friend.

At the pond, they splashed, and screamed in fun. It did not matter what they were doing, only that they were enjoying being kids. Amara was not afraid anymore and stopped to allow this feeling to fill her. She looked up to the sky and wondered if this feeling would last. Amara did not have a religion, not knowing why she looked to the sky. In this moment she was feeling something divine.

At sunset they all head over to the kitchen to eat with the rest of the kids. Thien was now like her guide. As they got closer they saw Joan helping feed everyone. Amara caught her eye. Joan saw her with the others, this made her very happy as she continued to serve up supper. It was simple and modest but at least it didn't have bugs in it, she thought. It was in an environment that was happy so the food tasted good. For the first time since Amara met these girls, all were quiet. All seemed to have the same feeling of appreciation for this meal. With out needing to speak it, they all understood. The girls in these places had developed their own language and ceremony that can not be

explained. It is like they are family or religion without name or instruction. They all understood without words. They all knew with out explanation. Far be it for anyone else to know what it was or to understand it.

******

Once they finished eating all the girls cleaned their table and bowls. They did not stop until each and everyone was clean and put away. Once done Amara went to Joan and asked if there was anything else she could do? Joan smiled and told her to go enjoy being a girl. Amara ran to catch up with the other girls and went into the bedroom. She was slow to enter. There lingered a haunting feeling of her room in the brothel. Thien saw this and called to Amara. She told Amara that she felt the same way when she first came here. She reminded her that this was not that place. She instructed her to let go of that old memory and join in on their fun. She could now sleep with out fear except for maybe the girl above her might pee the bed and wake her up.
They laughed and talked late into the night until everyone fell deeply asleep.

Just after sunrise, all were up and in the kitchen to eat. After that they followed the same routine.
An older woman approached Amara and invited her to morning circle. The woman was rather tall and pale. She wore plain clothes and a gold cross around her neck. She seemed soft spoken and kind. Amara agreed and walked with her to the place she saw when she entered the center. There were already 9 girls sitting in a circle. Some were happy while others were sad. Amara took a seat in the circle. The Nun made the introductions and asked who would like to speak first. There were no volunteers so she selected one. The girl sat with her head down in tears.

No one said a thing. Some also dropped their little heads, remembering what they went through. Amara looked at those around her and remembered what Mom told her about being there for others and not just herself. Tears of compassion flowed down her cheeks and she did not wipe them away. She felt safe here. No need to control what was going on. They all sat and waited for the Nun to do something. She moved to the girl and hugged her. Amara saw this and joined in the hug. Individually they made it a big group hug. The one asked to speak, sobbed loudly, many of the others joined in. After some time had passed they all recovered to a point. The nun stood and smiled.

Another girl from the courtyard walked over and greeted the Nun. They hugged and the girl said she would like to talk to them. The Nun agreed and introduced her to the group, "This is Mia, she is 15 years old, here for 3 years and would like to talk to all of you".

Now with the attention on this new girl it seemed the others began to relax. Mia told the girls that she wanted to share her experience with them. They would learn they are not alone in that which caused their suffering. As she began to speak, she paused, and looked down at the ground. Then smiling, she looked up and showed her strength. She showed that she owned her life now.

She began her message, "I have my own story, maybe it is like yours, maybe it is not but that makes no difference here. We have all been taken and made to do things that we did not want to do. I want you all to know that what they did to us was wrong. You are not to blame for being forced to do these awful things. It is not your fault. I am telling you the truth. I am you, you are me. I spent a long time here with people telling me it was not my fault.    In my

mind I kept wondering if it was something I did or did not do that made my family send me away to hell where we have all been. I am here to tell you that there is nothing on this earth that would make any of these experiences we had our fault. . ."

She continued, "My name is Mia and I am 15 years old and my parents were very poor. When I was 12 my father took me to a man's hotel room. The door shut. I yelled and screamed to get out of the room but the man there grabbed me and put his hand over my mouth, around the waist and told me to shut up or he would kill me. He had a knife and put it to my throat and pressed it against me. Then he did very bad things to me for a long time and all I could do is cry. When he was done he left the room with the door open. I ran to the village chief and told him what happened. He did not do anything but smile at me because the man had given him some money. I ran home and my parents would not talk to me. I knew they sold me for money to buy food. In the days to come my neighbors said bad things to me. I hated myself and tried to kill myself many times but could not go through with it. I hated everything and everybody. I told my auntie about what had happened and she took me in. She gave me food and love but I wanted my parents. Auntie explained that it would happen again and that I should never return. She explained that I needed to forgive them because they just wanted to eat. I felt so bad. I lost all my dreams about who I could be. Auntie told me she was going to take me to this place we are at right now. I did not want to go but I did not want to stay either. So she brought me to this place where I met Joan who was a little scary." A few of the older girls giggled.

Mia continued, "They gave me food and a place to sleep. Soon I found friends or I should say they found me. When I went to school here I learned many things about life and

how to support my self when I am an adult and leave this place. When I have bad memories about my past I go to my counselor, the Nun who smiles and hugs me. She helped me with my social skills and to discover what I want to do and where I want to go. I found my dreams again.  Not my old ones but new and big dreams. I learned here that I can be anything I want to be. You know I believed her and she was right. I studied many things here and went to the big city and discovered that I could do anything I wanted to do. Then I really missed this place, my new family, all of you."

Then Mia looked at each one of her "sisters" in the eyes.

She went on to conclude by stating, "If you have problems in your life then you face them. Be strong, you have support now. You get to be in control now. This place will always be your home. Always. Ok that is all I had to say." The little girl who was first asked to speak gets up and runs to her. She grabs her and holds her tightly. Mia smiles, lets go and tries to walk away
but now has a little girl attached to her. She asks her if she would like to help her in the garden to gather some food. The girl nods her head up and down and they move that direction. Mia does not seem to mind her tiny attachment as they go.

*******

Amara continued to go to the group and found many other activities to involve herself with at the center. She cooked in the kitchen, studied in school and spent much of her time at the pond. She learned how to be alive again. She was different than most of the girls who would come and go from this place. She seemed to have been waiting for this

time in her life to happen. With that came deep appreciation for this place and people that made it her family, her heaven. Amara would go on to leave this place and become a lawyer with the intention to return and help. She could go do anything now but here where she found herself was where she wanted to be. These rescue missions fight each day with having enough food or finding someone to repair the simplest things for free. Everything is donated here and somehow they get through.

Amara walks the streets looking for other girls who need help. She does what she can but it is dangerous to interrupt the flow of money that makes all of this a grim reality in our world. She has the three things needed to continue: faith, hope and love.

She realizes that the center is one day away from closing, one day away from someone not wanting it there, one day away from running out of food. Amara would not allow that into her reality. Amara would not allow that when she was sold by her Mom and Auntie, she did not allow that when she was beaten, tortured, and abused. She would not allow it now. The truth is that all these missions have to face this and that this dark part of our world is not wanted to be seen or talked about. People rather put it out of their mind and pretend it does not exist. The one thing that I know is that this problem will not go away and angels like Amara and Joan and so many others will spend their lives in the servitude to these kids. Amara is just one story of so many and for me I will not let this go unknown for the rest of my life. Once you have looked into the eyes of one of these children, you are never the same again. People often ask, why did God allow this to happen?   I respond, to give us the opportunity to do what we came here for, be human and learn what it means to be human. To help those in need

and hope that when we need it, someone will be there for us.

# Chapter 5

## In the Mind of a Sex Tourist

To understand the mind of a Sex Tourist one has to clear judgment in order to hear what is being said. I am not validating what they do. I am telling you direct conversations with some of these people. What I am about to share is hard to hear due to its graphic nature. I do not know of any where that anything like this in its completeness is available. I allow for you to be the judge of what you hear. In my life the thing that kept me alive and sane was the truth. It led to the success in capturing many violent criminals. No matter how disgusting what you are about to read is, it will let you know what people like me have to deal with in rescuing these children. 99% fail at what I do because they cannot accept this knowledge and still deal with these beasts. You may or may not have had to "walk in the valley of the shadow of death", and if you have maybe you did not make it back. God is good right? Well when one is confronted with evil in this reality it changes the choices they make. Each time one converses with one of these "tourists" a piece of the soul is lost. Many resort to prayer, or ceremony, both good but still passive. However some things on this earth must be faced and overcome. Slavery is one of these things. Maybe that is where I fit into all of this. I am successful at what I do where others fail. I apologize now for all those who I offend, but this must be written and it must be read.

One day while enjoying my coffee in a small Cambodian café I looked around to see many other travelers sitting by

themselves reading newspapers, checking phones and so on. It was my first time here and assumed it was a popular place for old guys from other countries. After all there were international newspapers to read and cream for your coffee, that sort of thing. It has become one of my hobbies to sit and watch people go about their day in these developing countries.

While caught up in observing my surroundings I noticed a young boy talking to one of the old guys who had been sitting by himself. Well that is weird I thought, perhaps they knew each other. Or perhaps it is not uncommon for older folk and younger to flirt here. Perhaps the generation gap hook up is quite acceptable here. Yet this boy looked too young for that. The man smiled a lot as the boy stood up and pulled at him to follow. Interesting I thought, but who am I to stick my nose into this? They left. Soon after another young boy came in and got the attention of two plump older guys in the corner. I watched as they laughed and carried on awhile. I also observed those who were running the café seemed to se this all as normal daily activity. Not long after, the two foreign men left with the boy. I tend to stay a long time, drink plenty of coffee and smoke my cigars freely. I tip well, like an hourly charge to the restaurant. This way they do not mind me and most of the time they become friendly with me. This allows me to break customs and ask questions that others would not dare.

As the day progresses on, I head out. Unintentionally I am following one of the other guys from the café. I feel inspired to follow him further and see what he is up to. I do not suggest anyone else do this. As I follow it seems he knows where he is headed and what he is looking for. I stall in a little shop, looking at the trinkets they have for sale like smokes, candy and canned drinks. Many locals have these as a way of providing income for the house. I see my

man talking to a young boy. Hmm, starting to see a pattern here. They walk off and head into one of the narrow alleys. I decide to follow and see where it takes me. Bad vibes fill me, still I persist. We go down many alleys and different directions. I forgot to bring skittles to find my way back. I see them enter a shanty house. All the "houses" are all connected in one way or another. I had been to some gambling homes before. Once inside you never really knew which way was out. All the
structures seemed to be interconnected, enclosed like a maze. I walk in their direction as a teenage boy comes to greet me. Come in sir he says, in his chopped up English. I said why, he smiled and pulled me by the arm. My curiosity makes me succumb to his persistence. So I concluded that I must follow or this may not work out so well for me.


Once inside I hear the other guy negotiating a price for a girl. Intuitively I knew this must be what was going on in the shadows here, but did not want to corrupt my vacation.

What I saw next, practically knocked the wind out of me, and that is not easy to do.

I witnessed a pin of kindergarten aged children all reaching for me and yelling to take them.

My stomach did a flip.

At that moment the other guy saw me and said with a smile, "heaven right?"

I nodded my head and looked away. The boy who brought me in asked me to choose one. I asked
how much and he said pick one first. The old guy looked over at me and told me not to pay any more than $40, they

try to get more but that is what they will always take. I felt out of balance as I tried to move my mouth with speech. I somehow managed to ask the boy if they had any who were older. He questioned, "boom boom"? So I answered, "yes, boom boom."

He grabs me by the arm and walks me past the kids as they all smile and reach for me like puppies in a pound. We walk down the hall to an opening and into another house. In there, are not so excited young girls that range in age from 12 to 15. I can see they all put on a faint smirk. I tell the boy I did not know that this place was for, hoping to open a way out for me. He looked at me and smiled real big, saying yeah yeah… you like? ! I believed he was calling my bluff and waiting for a reaction. I knew I could not be long in my reply, I had to make him happy. Along the way in the house I saw older men that were not customers. I knew they were enforcers. It is something you pick up on, living the life I have. I replied to the boy that I was happy he found me but still I was not ready.

He looked at me and asked if I was going to come here often?
He reminded me it was heaven, pure heaven.
Interesting how well he said the word heaven.
(When all the rest of his dialect was difficult to understand, although easy to follow).

I felt I had an out now if I played the game right. I asked if I could take them to my hotel. He replied, "Here, you stay here". He said I had to stay here if I wanted to visit heaven. I told him it
was dirty here and I was shy. I asked if I could pay more to take them to my hotel room? He looked around to see who was listening. Then he said the word, expensive. Again, I asked, how expensive? He still insisted that I choose one. I

reinstated that it was not going to happen right now. Again he insisted I pick one. So I picked one but could not look at her in the face. I felt what I was experiencing was 100% evil and that I was playing a game with the devil. So I just picked the one nearest me. The boy pushed her next to me and said you want. I showed the boy I had the authority here because he was starting to force this issue. I knew it was the only way he would hear me. I told him to give me a fucking price. He started to read my energy and said at hotel? Yes asshole I take to hotel… maybe…what price. Simultaneously I notice two shadows enter the room and stay along the wall. I looked over at them and told them, your boy it messing with me. I told them in louder voice to tell him to make up his mind. Inside I was growing in fear knowing this is not the way it works.  At the same time I had no intention of buying a girl unless it was to free her. It worked and the enforcers, not sure if they knew what I said but knew what I was expressing. I should have been an actor. One of them yelled at the boy and he said to me pick one. My eyes grew big and I ask the question again. He knew the answer all along and said $60 short time, $100 long time. I knew what he meant, short time was visit and go away, long time was overnight. I gruffly said thank you and that I would return. I turned to thank both enforcers and I got my ass out of there!

I did not look back!
My ploy worked!
I scampered the way I was led in and kept on scampering.
Was I being followed?
I dare not look back to find out.
I continued going until my emotions returned.
I was lost.
I took three consecutive lefts until I could hear the road.
Ah, the sweet liberating sound of traffic.

Back on the main street, I ducked into the first available bar.
Sitting, watching, looking, listening.
Had anyone velcrowed themselves to me?
For 60 minutes I nursed a draft.
So far nothing seemed to be connected to me.
I got lost in people watching again.
This time it was different.
Later in the evening.
The single male traveler stood out easily.
Now that I realized their purpose here.
It did not originally occur to me to pay it much attention.
I assumed everyone here was like me,
A connoisseur of organic raw culture.
I was fascinated by the life here,
All the things we take for granted back home.
Sit down toilets, showers without buckets, TV, internet and so on.
Why would anyone come to a place like this?
Back in my motel, I napped so I could be alert for the nocturnal activities.

I awoke from a nightmare only to realize I was not dreaming. I now knew the truth and did not want to feel it. I saw first hand what I had not wanted to see. This was my little town of meditation where I came to escape the world and experience a simple life. That is life, the yin and yang, the black and white, the good and evil. We develop our preferences and become what we want to be within the duality. The key is in embracing truth and not avoiding it. Choose the side you want to live on. Once accepted this it makes the evil worse and the good better than you can imagine. What a waste to come here and not really be here.

I changed clothes and head down for a coffee and a stroll around. Day and night here were vastly different worlds

here. Once at the café, it seemed my usual table was waiting for me. My coffee arrived and I closed my eyes in gratitude and thought. Then someone tapped my shoulder. Startled I looked up to see a familiar yet unfamiliar face. It was surprisingly the man I followed to the brothel yesterday. He said hello and introduced himself as "Dan". He asked to join me and so I agreed. I needed to understand more about this newly discovered evil. Here in my face was a piece of its' puzzle. I could have raged at him, told him what I thought of him, chased him away or worse. How would that serve anything but momentary relief? I decided if this was something I could teach others or help with I needed to know what the face of the enemy looked like. This seemed to be a start. There are those that talk but I tend to be the one that walks. If you are going to talk about something or have a view I think you should have the authority to do something. To have that authority you need to become that fragment of life. So he sat and it seemed he thought we were friends now. Partners in crime. So I let the conversation flow and participated as much as I could to get him to open up.

I wanted to know him....

"So how did it go Dan?" I quietly asked.

"Nice, buddy... real nice." He replied.

"How so Dan?" I asked further.

The waiter interrupted us. He wanted to serve us. I told him my usual and get my new buddy Dan a beer. The waiter knew me and looked at me without a smile. I winked at him and touched his arm. He knew then I was not my new buddy's friend. He cracked a smile but it vanished as soon as he knew it was showing.

know how to use it. I got the temperature right and soaped her down. I never use that crap the motel gives you. I get the good stuff from the store it really lathers up and you have to scrub it off. Now that really is fun, you feel me buddy"?

"Oh yea I feel you, (thinking to myself how I would like to feel his torture)", were my words and thoughts.

Dan went on to say, "At first I had to help her but eventually she got it you know. Damn, when she was washing my cock I thought I was going to lose it so I made her stop. I had not even taken my pill yet. You know I like to take my time and really get going before I do it. Anyway you know their holes are not all the way formed yet, I am not sure but sure feels good. Needless to say it did not take long before I exploded". Then he laughed.

I wanted to barf but somehow continued my interview, "So, that was it Dan?"

"No way, I got her to put on her top and skirt with no underwear. Total school girl fantasy. I pretended to be her teacher and she was my student as I touched her body. I got her on the bed on her hands and knees and lifted her skirt. I really wanted in that back door, but once she knew what was happening she resisted. That really turned me on. I grabbed her by the back of the neck and forced her down so she could not move. That is what is so great about these little things, you can control them. They know that the boss will beat them if they do not obey. So she settled down and I did the deed. I never could get it all the way in. They are so tight you know. I didn't even use lube. It did not seem to matter anyway, I was so turned on that I lost my wad in a matter of minutes. Once I was complete, I wanted her to leave. That is the other great thing here, when

it's over you can tell them to scram. I gave her an extra two bucks. I know that always makes them happy. That's a lot of money to them you know. Then I got into the shower and washed that slim off. They are so dirty you know, that was probably the first shower she had in a week".

Then he laughed again. "You know the damn thing is that once you live out these fantasies, with in a few hours you want it again. Like Chinese food you know, addicting. All it takes is a shower, a short nap and I am thinking about it again.

Then I run into you, I never did get your name." he finished.

"Z", I answered.

"Z? That is all?" he asked.

"Yes, that is it." I said curtly.

"Ohhhhhh, I get it, for real though! It is best that peeps don't know who you really are!" he exclaimed. He laughed and shook my hand. Then he had a question for me, "So buddy how was your bitch?"

"Oh I kind of freaked out and left. But I did it calmly. They expect me back. I Did not want to close any doors." I explained.

"Why would you not have fun dude? I am telling you, you will never regret it, but you might get addicted." He said with a smile.

"Yeah, but what about the police?" I questioned like a chicken.

"Dude they own them." He reassured me.

"No shit," I said.

"Yep, no shit. Just another reason why it is heaven man, pure heaven here," he added.

Again that reference, I could swear my eyes turned red but I managed to control myself.

"Maybe you can give me a tour Dan. I need to understand I am not going to get into any trouble," I said.

"Dude, as long as you keep it on the down low. You know, don't be too public. There are people around here that take pictures of us. Not sure why but it makes me feel a bit uneasy," said Dan.

"I can understand that" I sympathized.

"It is part of the game you know. So I can take you around and show you some of the street pussy and some of the clubs. Don't worry. They will make you feel comfortable and put you at ease." boasted Dan.

"Ok, I will buy the taxi", I agreed.
We got a taxi and Dan knew the driver. Seemed very friendly and they chatted it up as we drove. Dan slid back and forth on the seat talking to the driver and having a good time talking about their conquests. It was like they were talking about sports. Inside I was turning, I just did not know what to think, was this real? I never had a problem with adults in prostitution or brothels to a point. It was after all a timeless profession and it may never end, but this was far different. These were little children treated worse than animals, with zero kindness.

As we drove the driver would slow down and point out new brothels and some girls walking along the street. I asked Dan about the ones on the street and he explained they ranged in age from 13-16. They were too timid to leave the brothels so the owners allowed them to bring in costumers from the outside. The real cash is in selling the little ones, but they pose the greatest risk at running away, so they keep them tight under lock and key.

There are wars amongst the brothels to steal girls from each other. Inside the buildings and bars are the line ups. You pick your girls and take them into the room with the karaoke machine. In there you can order beer or food and have sex with the girls. These girls are older but the rules are basically the same. When I say older I mean 14 to early 20s. We stop at a little bar and get out. Dan says, "free ride, he knows me well".

*******

We go into this tiny bar that sets in the middle of several larger bars and get a beer. This is where we can sit and scope out the action and see if any of the picture takers are here. Then he tells me about the taxis.

"You know that cabbie is your best friend here. He is your ticket to anything you want", Dan says.

"How so", I ask?

"They are connected to all the people here for drugs, girls, boys or whatever you are into", Dan explained.

"This one trip I came here and stuck to the bars and had my fun then one night after I took a girl back to my room I

he rejoined us and he too had a big smile on his face. Chuckling at me he wanted to know what I thought. Then he chuckled again, saying there was no need for an answer, he could see it on my face. So we left and went back to the bar and the police went on his way. The cabbie told me that I was "In" now. He called me his friend and said to be respectful to the police when I saw them. Cabbie took me to the bars like I will with you and show you how it works, don't worry it is not rocket science" Dan concluded.

We finished our beer and he patted me on the back. We went a few doors down to another open air club with girls dancing half heartedly around. They were totally not into it, but this was their job so they did it. All of them had a number on their dress like someone running a track race. I think the average age was about 16. Everyone in the club seemed to know Dan, saying hello as they passed by, even the other foreigners all seemed to know Dan. It was like a boys club. The men appeared to be from many different countries. The manager came over to us and I was introduced and now I was part of the boys club, oh great. The manager sat next to me and asked what I thought of his place.

I told him, "So many beautiful girls, all so young".

"Yes they are, to keep you young my friend. They will do whatever you ask. Yes, but don't hurt them too much. Ok. Then we have a problem. I need them to work." He said with a smile.

"Where you find these girls" I asked?

"Oh they come to me all time. They want work. They can earn good money here." he said.

"Really, I got the impression they didn't make much and were confined to small rooms." I challenged.

"Oh, ha-ha, you talk about those dirty brothels. Stay away my friend no good, you come here.   My girls want to be here. They take care of their families. I pay real good. You can ask any of them." He said.

"I will", I said with authority in my voice.

"Ah you funny guy, you look so serious." He joked.

Thinking I better calm down a little I poked him in his side and laughed.  The manager got up and pointed at a few girls to join us.  They approached and sat on our laps and touched our hair playfully. Their English was decent as they asked if we loved them. I smiled and complimented her outfit. I looked over at Dan who was all smiles. Then he said, "Hey Z, check out how firm these breasts are! Heaven right"!

The girl smiled and let him fondle and squeeze her like he was buying fruit at the market.

I gave him the thumbs up while I choked inside. The girl with me started to get a little too
friendly so  I grabbed her hand. She asked me to buy her a drink and I knew what that meant.    It was not going to be a real drink but some high priced watered down liquid so the bar could make money. I agreed and we waited. Dan now was getting real friendly with the girl on his lap and she stopped his hand as it got lower. So I guess there is a limit.

Dan yelled to me over the music, "Hey Z, you like your girl? Let's go!"

I replied, that I liked her just fine. Then we paid the waiter and all got up from the table. Dan had two girls on his arms and we walked out. The girl that was with me followed and reached for my hand. I realized what Dan meant; we were taking the girls out!

Now what am I going to do? I am not going to do what is expected. I must take her to different room and talk with her if she is willing. Dan explained we could get a room for about six bucks across the street and so we did. His face looked disappointed when I paid for a separate room, but he assumed that I was shy. After we entered our room, the girls face changed. This was a job to her so she started to undress. I stopped her and sat her down at a chair. I sat next to her and asked her name. She told me it was "Star". I assumed this was not her real name but she smiled and said it was the name her parents gave her. I smiled back and told her that I only wanted to talk. I had to reassure her that she would be paid the same wages, which came to $15.00.

I said very calmly to her, "I will pay you $60 if you promise not to tell anyone we only talked".

She quietly answered, "Ok, yes sir. Why"?

I explained, "I am not one of these guys and I really don't like them. I don't want anyone to know because I want to learn about this".

Shyly she asked why I wanted to learn.

"Because the truth really is hard to find here, everyone lies", I answered.

"Yes sir, I am ashamed my country. When you pay me sir"
she said.

I handed her the money and asked if he was hungry. Her
eyes got big as she smiled and said yes!

"Should we go eat", I questioned?

Star said that not all the restaurants let her eat in them
because she worked at the bar. She said there was one place
with good food and nice people and so we went.

"What about your friend" she asked?

"I am sure he is too busy to worry about me" I said and she
laughed with a sigh of relief.

As we left the room, I turned in the key as we exited. As
we walked out into the street there was a white woman
taking a picture of me and the girl who had my arm. Star
pulled me away from her and I stopped her and told her it
was ok. We posed for the woman who looked angrily at us.
I tried to approach her but she moved away quickly. I
wanted to invite her with us to eat. I thought maybe she can
teach me about this also. As of now that would not happen
as she ran away. So Star and I made our way down the
street to find the restaurant she wanted to eat at. I could feel
her excitement as we went in. The owner smiled when he
saw her and looked at me with a snarl. Star introduced me
and told him I was not one of them. Suddenly he smiled
and was very welcoming. It was nothing fancy and just like
most of the open aired restaurants lining the streets. This
one was clean though.  I asked Star to order for me and she
asked what she could have. I laughed and told her anything
and as much as she wanted. Her eyes grew really big as she

hastily placed our order. When she came back and sat next to me, it hit me, that she thinks
I want to be her boyfriend or something so I should clarify my intentions.

"Star, I want to make it clear that I just want to be your friend and not your boyfriend." I said.

Star smiled and said no problem, if I fed her well she will be my best friend. We laughed.

"How did you learn English so well" I asked?

"I learn by listening to people and one man gave me a book about it" she said.

"Wow you speak so well" I complimented her.

"Thank you" she said.

"Star, will you be open to me and answer my questions? Don't worry only I will know what we talk about. It is just so I can understand this life you have and the other girls" I explained.

"Why you want to know? So boring" she yawned.

"I am not sure why I want to know. It is not boring to me because this is all new to me" I said.

"Sure anything you want sir" she agreed.

"Good" was my final word.

The food came and there was not much talking because the food was evaporating at the table. My goodness this girl

was hungry! She was not what I was expecting and seemed so normal. I found out she was 16 and had been doing this for two years. The owner came to the table as we were eating and asked if I liked the food.  We started to talk and he was interested in who I was and why I was with Star. It was a friendly line of questioning. I felt from his energy I could tell him what I was doing with her and how that came to be. He understood and his face became long.  I could tell he really liked Star as a daughter. I learned that he had helped her many times to eat and some money to keep her from the brothel. He did not have a good opinion of what Star was doing but understood why she did it. There is no other way here for a girl to provide for her family. In this culture women are sub human and not worth anything because they are not strong and only take from the little resources a family has. The owner was different, he did not see things like the culture around him and I could tell he was a good man. He warned me to be careful because if others knew what I was doing they would not like me much and that would be dangerous. He said I would just disappear. Poof like bubble. Well by now Star was fat and I think ate 3 times her body weight.

I looked at the owner and asked if it was safe to talk here. He advised we go walk by the park
where no one would pay attention to us. Star agreed and we left the restaurant. I have made a new friend in the owner and I am sure I will be back to eat at his place. It is always good to have friends in places like this. As we walked I could not help but see her as my daughter, so young and alive. I do not have children but imagine this might be a little of what it would feel like.
I wanted to help and protect her, that sort of thing. This was not my culture and it is not my place to lay judgment or get involved in any way that interrupts this way. I realized that

I am just another John that is not having sex with her, I was here to learn. Star was quietly looking around,
she had my hand and was swinging it to and fro. I did not want to interrupt that so we continued to where the park was in silence. Well sort of, Star was singing a melody softly and quietly.
After about 10 minutes we reached the park that was next to the ocean and we sat on the concrete barrier.

She explained that her parents lived in a squatter's village on the sea. She had 4 older brothers and one younger sister. They would fish in the morning and bring back the fish to give to their mom. Then mom and Star would go to market and sell them.  Father could trade the fish for vegetables, soda or candy which they could take to market and make more money. Many times there were no fish and no money. They would have to borrow food from their neighbors. Many times if her father did not get fish it meant neither did the neighbors. Sometimes they would go days without food or rice. All the boys would find something they could do to get a little money, they needed to eat more than the girls. She felt lucky because many parents sold their daughters to the brothels and never saw them again. Sometimes they gave them away to anyone who wanted them. We never saw any of those kids again. Star dropped her head. It was effecting her
her heart to think about it. She wondered every day when her father would sell her. He never hurt her but he never really showed any love to her either. When she was 14 she knew other girls who sold themselves to the bars to help their families and give them a feeling of value.  So Star went with one of the other girls to the bar one night and decided to do this for her family. She told her mom and her mom did not say anything just looked away. She told her father too, he did the same. That is how it all started.

# Chapter 6

## In the mind of a sex tourist part 2

I slept very late today. Every time I woke up I wanted to sleep again and so I did. Depression was consuming me from most every direction and the distaste in my mouth made me sick. I really did not know why we should live life if it is really like this. How could people allow this to go on? Does the world not really know what happens in it? Is there a reality that others turn a blind eye to by choice? An obscured focus in life that builds in false importance, persuading others to believe it is right… I reflected on my life and saw its own comparisons. Was I one of the people to hear but not see or speak out? Did I live a life of distraction? Jobs, sports, friends, chasing love, so on and so forth. Did I perceive "bad things" happening "over there" in a far off world, when the truth was statistically it could be happening next door? I was beginning to understand and see the world around me as it really was…

I have been pushed, guided and struggled through life. Wondering if free will, fate or divinity was lighting my path as I went…I learned to melt and mold into becoming what those around me wanted to be. Educated, hard working, pursuing a cause, made me a good person, right? I felt I was no longer alone in my body, like a thousand people

without a leader or rules. I was realizing just how much potential I possessed. Like most, we think we are limited and unable to make a difference. What if we were to make a difference for even just one person's life? We can't own them for life, we must help others find their way. It seems others give help with so many conditions. Is that really giving? No it's not! You can not gift someone with money then make demands on what they do or do not spend it on. The only way to give is without condition. If the person does what you tell them, well that is just a perk of the giving. I'm thinking it is the same here, only instead of money it is humans. If I can physically save even one child, I changed a moment in time with out condition. This moment could have a ripple effect, thus saving thousands more. Hence, nothing could be more important than saving the one.

The depression faded as the answer became clear.

All of my worldly accomplishments began to fade into the background of the obsolete.

To save one person from hell, seemed worthy to me, even if it meant my last day alive doing it.

This was my life's quest, I had been preparing with out knowing it.

There was no definition, direction, or class I could take. The only way was through experience.

I collected many skill sets in life that served me on a temporary basis. Even the depression I felt became temporary as I soared to a high of realizing what I had discovered. While I still felt I contained a thousand spirits in one body, I believe I found their leader, ME!

All this made it possible to swim in the cesspool of Dan's version of life.
This was why I tolerated him with out stopping him.
I needed to know.

He led me to Star, my first positive step towards saving others like her.
So hypothetically they were saving my life.

Here I was on holiday from my work with the alphabet soup, looking to disconnect.
In reality my thousand spirits within led me to this point so I could lead.
I guess holiday has just been postponed and my new employer has work for me to do.
My new employer, being me, can be a real pain in the side once he activates passion.
So like it or not I prepared to learn more until something happened to ignite my talent to act.
I would go deep down the dark rabbit hole and see where it would take me.

I got up, head downstairs, and out the door. It was much later than my usual outings to sit in the café. I decided to roam and see what was up. As I pass by my waiter, I wave hello and he says hi. He asks where I was this morning. I smile and told him that I died, but today I was reborn. We chuckled as we parted ways. I hoped to avoid seeing Dan, as that would stop the flow, although I did not know where the flow was taking me. I walked with out direction until I ended up in a familiar location, the restaurant that Star took me to. The Owner saw me before I saw him. He remembered my name and asked if I was hungry. I was indeed, so I sat down.

I ate with the owner who introduced me to his wife. As we talked we got more into the life of Star and the life that is Cambodia. Again, I had to make it clear to him that my only interest in Star was as her friend. Still he wanted me to take her away from all this, so did his wife. I understood him and I think he understood me. Even still his wife acted as cheer leader for me to rescue Star from her life. It was almost comical to watch, had the subject not been so serious.

While we talked I thought about how I could help her even if little and temporary. They said she was next door sleeping off all the food she ate the night before. I asked the wife if she could bring her into the restaurant. A little while later, per usual for Asian time, they appeared at our table. I told her that I had an offer for her that I wanted her friends to be witness too.

"What offer", she asked?

My answer went something like this, "I want to hire you to be mine and only mine until I leave. I am not sure how long that will be, maybe a week or a month. Since I don't know I will add two weeks pay to that. What I mean to being mine is that you will not work at the bar and not go on any dates or anything related to that work. I will need you to be available to me if I want to talk or something that I may need you for. All this will be simple, no problems for you. Maybe if I need you I can come here and you can leave word with them where you will be so I can always find you. If you cheat on this the deal will be over right then and no extra pay. I know you were lying about how much money you make, I understand why you did and I don't care. So here is my offer: I will give you $20 USD per day, seven days a week".

The owner and his wife looked very happy and the wife pinched Stars arm. Star smiled and said ok. I don't think it was a very hard decision for her. So I shook her hand and gave her $20 and told her I would talk to her later if I needed her. I think to myself maybe or maybe not she will obey my rules but from what I have learned about this culture it is her duty to obey a man. I think knowing this information I can use it to my advantage in this way. Sometimes bad rules can be used for good roads. With that I walked out and headed down the street without direction. It was getting near dusk and night would soon cover the city. That is when all the vermin come out to "play". I suppose that is when Dan will show up. Maybe I need to see him but no loss if I don't. I walked 'til dark and was near all the bars now. I see ahead of me the Chief and he is walking straight for me. I put on a smile and act glad to see him. I know he will expect a thank you and so I oblige. He tells me that if there is anything I need I can come directly to him and don't have to see the cabbie or anyone else. He tells me I can trust him and if I see any trouble to go to him directly. I make him think I am on board and will be his little puppet so I can play without interference. The Chief goes on his way and I look around to see if anyone might be watching and what do I see but one of the camera people taking pictures of us. I wave and continue on my way.

As I walk along passing the bar I was in the other night I see a somewhat smaller one around the corner and so I decide to go in and see what is going on. I feel kind of weird because this is sort of odd for me, I don't know what I am looking for. I take a seat at the end of the bar a little out of the way and in a darker area. The music in these places is so loud and this seemed a good place to avoid much. I take a seat and get a beer. Then I hear a loud voice over the music and it is that piece of shit Dan. He shouted to me, calling me his buddy. He wanted to know if I was on

my own tonight. Said I would never be seen by the girls if I sat in the back.

I clenched my jaw. He asked where I left to the other night, said he went looking for me.

I asked firmly, "Why go looking for me, when you knew that I was busy"?

He sighed, "Ah you addicted now"?

"You know it Dan", was my short answer. Then I asked if he wanted to tell me some of his stories.

"Ok, you know I love sharing my experience, I will be your teacher", he giggled as he led me down the way to a place less crowded and noisy.

We take off and I leave my beer behind. The bar tender calls out for me and hands it to me. I did not know you can walk outside with a beer but I guess I don't know much of anything yet. So I grab it and thank him and off I go with my "buddy" Dan. We walk just a little way to another open air bar bigger than where we were but smaller than the place I met Star. We find our way to the outer edges nearer the street and take a seat. Dan excuses him self to the bathroom and brings
us back more beer. I pour the one I have out in one of the plants by the table, not really a good place or position for me to be drunk. As I sit there one girl after another walks by wanting my attention. I looked at one in the eyes and she immediately sat down. I understand now that if you want their attention you just look at them in the eye. She introduces herself. I tell her, sorry that seat is taken and I did not mean for her to sit. She gets up looking pissed and moves on. Dan now finds his way back to me with more

beer in hand and a really big smile. It is an odd feeling in my stomach because Dan really gives the impression of being a nice guy. If I had not met him here I might have become friends with him. But I am sure I would have figured him out eventually.

"So Z, how you like the other side of life here", he questioned.

"Well Dan, I understand your love of this place and before you found me I ran into the Chief and he was very nice to me. Gave me a feeling like it is ok here to do pretty much what I want as long as he has a hand in it", I answered.

"I told you that you will be fine here if you pay attention to the obvious rules. Just don't be an asshole unless you are being pushed. Then only push back as hard as you need to. Don't go over the top", he instructed.

"Think I got it. I'm not here to cause any trouble just enjoy what you call heaven", I assured him.

"Oh baby, this here is heaven. I knew you would enjoy this stuff", he exclaimed. Then he went on to "school" me further saying, "I have always liked the younger girls, you know the innocent
and naïve ones. When you date the older ladies they already know the game and they say no a lot. Just a real pain in the ass and life is difficult already! Besides that you have to spend so much time and money. So much money and they may not even put out. I dated two girls at one time who would not give me a blow job. Can you imagine? How in the world could I find two girls at
the same time that would not suck my dick", he said baffled.

"Damn, man that sucks", I say void of emotion.

"No, that is the point, hahah, they didn't", he complained. "Then I took a trip to the Philippines and went to the famous city, Angels City, you know where all the hookers are. There I started to hook up with these younger girls", said Dan.

"Did they suck you", I asked matter of fact.

"Hahaha, you bet! And to pay them was way cheaper than dating. Besides, that is all we want anyway right", he questioned. Then he explained how his buddies back home were all married dudes who bitched about their wives and complained about lack of sex and money. Even when they were getting along with their wives, they say their kids empty their pockets too", he explained.

"I get ya", I shrugged.

"So while hanging out in the Philippines I started to expand out to other places and found that these young girls here are always smiling at me and looking at me. You know me, instant hard on. Woo hoo! So I thought to myself I can get one of these girls to go out with me. Sure they will want some money or a new dress or phone or something you know. Hell why not I thought, its going to cost me one way or the other. So I was at the mall and I see this girl smiling at me and she was working at the department store in the jean department. I walk over and she so shy but asks if I want some jeans. I think I blushed at the moment and told her yes, but looking at her jeans made me want in hers", he went on.

"Bam! Can you believe that line worked? I gave her my cell number and she called that night. She was 15 and so fine, tight body and all, I really wanted her. So I took her out to a movie and we had some food at a nice place, well nice for the Philippines, and headed back to my room. I could not believe my luck. We got in the  room and she turned on the TV and laid back on the bed. I joined her and tried to take off her shirt but she did not want that but I could feel her up anyway. It was kinda like teasing you know and she opened the rest up to me", said Dan.

He went on to brag about how he saw her several times a week, even going to her shack of a house. There he met her father who thanked him for buying her clothes and being so nice. He said the dad was younger than he was. He also got to meet her sister who was 13 and "developed", whom he knew was going to be trouble. He went on in his bragging, "You know, I saw her a few days later in the town and bought her some ice cream. You are not going to believe this, I got her back to my room and like her sister she turned on the TV. I laid with her on the bed and after a couple of hours I started to feel her nice young body. You know I got HER to give me a blow job! It all comes back to you if you are patient. Well that did not end well because she told her sister and boy was she pissed. That ended that, I did not want drama. Drama is what we are avoiding right", he said in assumed solidarity.

He told me rather nonchalantly how he moved on and "went back the next day to another mall".
He said he was a little smarter now and knew not to get involved with sisters, but did find himself involved with best friends. He boasted about having many girlfriends there, still talking to some. All of them were under 18 and he didn't want "the hassle".

He educated me further on his next trip to Cambodia, stating that, "Back in the 1980's it was said that 100% of the girls were in the brothels on some level or another". He explained how things were different now due to child protection agencies that take your picture and register you. "They watch you and post you on websites and stuff. Some even black mail you and that usually cost you about $1000 if you play the game. I even heard of some guys that did not play and just disappeared. So you got to watch yourself man, seriously. If you get known with the brokers of the girls they help protect you. I think some of the black mailers are afraid of them. So it's a good thing to stay close to these guys".

"I started hanging out in the parks at dark. That is normal, many people go there. The parks are well lit but you can still find dark places if you are into that sort of thing. I found many girls between the ages of 14 and 16. I could buy for as little as $5 a night. They are a little less clean and not made up like the girls in the bars but they are younger. If you find a girl who is older, like 17 or 18 she is likely to have some disease so I would stay away from that if I were you. Besides the younger girls are so much more fun. If they say no they don't mean it and you can ignore them anyway. Sometimes if I wanted company, it was easy to take them into Vietnam or Thailand. It used to be pretty easy to get them a visa, but now it is a little harder. But I can still pass from Cambodia, Vietnam, and Laos. Sometimes it is nice to have a ripe young slave with you. If you can't find anything better there to squeeze, you can take her out of your suitcase! Hehehehehe", he chuckled to himself.

"Sounds like you just got it all don't you", I said in monotone.

He told me how he would keep coming back here forever. He justified that we deserved a life of happiness and in the process we made the females happy (most of the time). He said that with a little time and money the world could revolve around us. Dan raises his glass and wants to cheer so I comply. He sits back and with wide eyes looks around smiling and says, "Tonight I am looking for a little class and a firm little ass, I think I will buy one of these", he hissed.

"But they look 15 and older", I say.

"Ah 15 is alright but I see some that can't be more than 14", says Dan the man.

Soon after he motions one over to his lap and gets friendly. He encourages me to find one but I tell him not tonight. After buying the girl a drink they leave and he is all smiles. I have to leave also because my head is just not right after hearing all of Dan's layers of stories.

I want to erase my mind.

The next few days were spent hanging out at the café at my hotel drinking coffee. The waiter asks me what's wrong? He said I looked a little different, like I had changed or something. He
wondered if I was ill. So I asked if he knew Dan and he did. I think that was all he needed to hear to know why I was changed. He told me don't think of it. I can't escape it and there are other things to think about. I smiled and agreed to him but in my head there was no escape but what could I do. I wanted to talk to Star more and I am sure she is wondering if I am going to pay her. So I leave and walk down to the restaurant she is accustomed to. I see the owner and he is happy. I ask him about Star and he sends one of

the kids outside to go get her. We have pleasant conversation until she arrives in smiles and sits down. We order some food and I ask her to go talk with me at a park and of course she agrees.

As we walk for a while I notice that Star is not the happy girl I saw the last time so I asked her what was wrong.

"Z, I was thinking, what am I going to do when you leave", she asked with sadness in her sweet voice.

I stay silent and I find no answer for her.

"When you go, I will have to go back to my work at the bar and I don't want to. I hate it but it supports my family and now they accept me. I bring money and it makes it easier for my sister. If they have no money I don't know what they will do", Star pleaded.

"What do you mean", I asked with compassion.

She explained how all the girls end up like this, families need to eat, it is how it is around here.
She said how her neighbors would look down on her for the work she does, even her family does not accept her job but they take the money just the same. She told of how her working protects her younger sister from the same fate.

I gave her my sympathies and said that I did not have an answer because I did not understand her culture. I asked about the other girls I see around town who get to work in a restaurant or store. Why could she not do these jobs? She explained how most of those girls were married or had family with money to live well.

"Maybe you will get married if you stop working in bars", I suggest humbly.

"No, I am trash, I am already ruined. Girls like me don't get married. I don't want to anyway", was her answer. "Besides it is just the same without money. Girls that get married here still have to bring in money to give husband and husband will beat you if you do not bring in enough money for him", she said with discouragement.

"How much is enough money", I inquire.

"Depend on man and what he wants", she answers.

"What could he want", I ask?

"Sometimes man good but, you do not understand. If I am woman I am not the same. Maybe he gamble, drink or want to buy girl for night. That is man. We all have to know our place", she said.

"You are right, I do not understand. If you could do anything you want what would that be", I asked.

"Anything that would feed me and let me not get beat anymore", was her heartfelt reply.

I had a lot to say to her but I held back because I really don't understand this culture. But I also understand breaking the system. I have seen the devastation left by missionaries and large charity organizations that come in and change lives for the better then when the money runs out they have to leave and when they do the people have lost their old ways and the new way disappears. You can't change the culture but you can teach skills and let them find the way. The reason most of these good hearted people

and companies fail is they do not understand the culture to start with. They think like what they know. I could sit here and preach to Star about how she is an equal and she deserves more. I can encourage her to stay positive but that talk has zero meaning here. This is a man's world and if you are a female you learn to be seen and not heard, while you hope for peace in your own world. If you are a woman and stand up there is no one that will help you when they come for you. It matters not if you are right or wrong. That is just the way it is. I could support her for some time but to what end. There are almost all the girls here in the same situation. I'm not rich and I can only do so little, right? There has to be a way.

"Star I know that just accepting your situation will not change it. I also know that there is a way that you just have not found yet. Maybe you have to ask people for help", I said compassionately.

She stops in her tracks and stares at me saying, "No one help anyone here, it is what has to be. Both have to use each other. You cannot trust anyone. I tried and it always is bad. Nothing does not cost anything".

"You trust me", I say curiously.

"No", she says with conviction.

"Why? I ask for very little, just talk and I pay you well", I reassure her.

"You pay me but what then, I still wait to see. Are you going to save me and take me to your country? Are you going to give me a lot of money and leave and expect me to be devoted to you. How you save me Z, how", she pleaded.

"I did not say I would. I ask for talk, and I pay you", was all I could commit to.

"And you tell me not to work in bar while you pay me", was her voiced concern.

"Yes, I stand corrected", I said, then added, "What if you could work somewhere and have good place to live and have plenty of food everyday"?

"I need the money for my family more than I need the food for myself", was her reply.

I scratched my head thinking. My wheels were turning at rapid speed. I told Star that I had to go and would find her again soon. With that I walked away, I had an idea. I head back to the restaurant to see the owner and his wife. I have a solution and wonder why no one had thought of this before. Maybe I am wrong but sometimes something so simple is not seen because of the complications of life. I walk fast to get to the restaurant and find the owner. Although I just ate a half hour ago, the owner insists I buy more food. He wants to know if I lost Star. I explained that she was still in the park where I left her to come and talk to them. He smiled suspiciously as he served me the food, then went to fetch his wife. Five minutes later they returned, looking confused as to why I want to talk to them. I compliment them on their cooking. I mention that they must have to wake early to go get this wonderful food.

"Yes and sometimes have to go back to market if we are very busy. But sometimes it takes so long to find any fresh left", they told me.

"So you work all the time everyday huh", I ask.

"Yes", they said with a deep sigh.

"And you, Mom you take care of so many kids and still have to help husband with restaurant", I ask.

"Yes, you know the kids so young", she answered.

"Sir, do you get the best deal at the market", I inquire further.

"It is hard because I don't have the time to get there for auction price. I have to take what I get", he answered.

"Why don't you hire someone to buy for you or buy from those that deliver everyday", I asked?

"I have good restaurant and people expect what I serve. I also have many foreigners who come here every time they visit Cambodia", was his reply.

"Do you love Star", I cut to the chase. I look at both of them and see the confusion on their faces.
"I know you love her and try to help her when you can", I say from the heart.

The eyes of the wife tear up as she explains, "You know Z, I wish life was different. I see Star as a daughter but I can only do so much. She is such good person always try to help me and is so nice to my family. She even brings customers to our restaurant. I know she has such good heart. I wish we could do more but we can not".

So I shared my idea, "What if you buy your fish from Star? Have her go in morning and other times when you need it. She can buy much cheaper than you and you can teach her what you want. Pay her the difference of what you save.

Maybe charge just a little more for it from your customers. A little will not be noticed by customers but the more meals your serve it will add up. I understand this will not save you much money but you will always have good product. She can also run errands that you have to leave to do. She can also wait on people and clean things you have not had time for. With this she can also help you Mom to take care of kids give you a break and let you and your husband be with each other more. If you want to. Haha. So Star could stay with you in your place and you could feed her. She would have safe place and stay away from bars and help her family with the money. You can give her money for buying the fish and selling to you. Your family would have a lot of help that you do not have to pay for. Just give her a place to sleep and feed her. I hope I am not wrong to suggest this. I am sorry if so, I am only thinking of how everyone can win".

They sat and looked at each other for awhile and said nothing. I began to think I broke a rule with this culture. I noticed the wife looking up to her husband like a kid asking for a toy. That is the best way I could describe it. Holding hands and just looking at each other. Then the owner looked at me, asking if Star wanted to do this job?

"I don't know, when this thought came to me I left her and came straight to you", I exclaimed.

Wife chimes in, "I will go find her"!

I say that it is time for me to go too and wish them all well. Everyone seems happy. I remind them to tell her that I will continue to pay her while I am here and will come to talk to her again.

"You are going to leave? You don't want to stay and see what she says", they say in unison.

"I think all has been said on my part. I do want to know but I think this is your life and like she said I will leave someday soon. Bless you sir for considering this, I worry that I could not make a difference", I said as I left.

Back at my hotel I felt different somehow. I wondered if Star would accept and if the owner and his wife would be able to work with her. There is so little trust here. Women don't think anything can be better and they have this duty to their family. I am not in a position to judge but I can have my opinion. I feel hopeless and I feel I am in a place of hopelessness. Maybe this event will be a success and spirit will give me other ideas of how to make a positive influence. I got to my room and fell to bed asleep. I did not know what I would do with the rest of my days here or if I would just bug out tomorrow. Well maybe I will have some answers when I wake.
With the dawn of first light, I was up and in the shower. Soon I was down at the café for morning coffee hoping for answers in my brew. My waiter quickly brought me a hot cup and a piece of French bread. He smiled and said no charge.

There really are good people here but a lot of bad also. I don't think some of the bad know it. After some good sleep I know nothing is hopeless but in this place I know it is a challenge. I also know it is not just this place but all of Asia. Now what to do is the question. I have more contract work available if I choose or I can stay here and think how one person can make a difference without being killed or something worse. Is it worth it to try with all the odds against you. What to do with Dan and should I even try, he has been a great teacher, I think. Or did he open my mind to

what I now I understand is the reason so many that learn of this world close off any further thought and go on their life. I think they go on with their life.

# Chapter 7

## Ecuador

With my new experience it was time to return to what I knew as normal for me, mercenary work.

This time my occupation would take me to Ecuador. Seems an oil tycoon found him self kidnapped for ransom. This is where most of a soldier for hire's income derives. Large corporations send employees to work in these less than modern countries and sometimes they don't come back. They discover the wages earned were not enough and find other ways of collecting it. The corporation contracts our team to resolve the situation. Normally it is a matter of negotiating a price. This time was a bit more complicated, they seemed very unreasonable, we

knew we were going to have to take it to the next level. This usually leads us to the exact person we need to talk to, not some "go-between" who does not have the authority to effect change. So we gift some money to the rif raf in the streets. When they get the impression that their life is about to be shortened they gather loose lips. When we get a solid lead we encounter the law enforcement. We make our presence known to the legitimate sources of intelligence we seek. If it is not a good lead they show us in how they react to our intimidation. If they are the source we seek they also give us the indication that identifies them as who we seek. Once confirmed we act and it is not long then that we have the leads that take us directly to the kidnapped employee.

Once there we go into 24 mode: asses, plan, act, extract and go home in 24 hours.

So that is how it went, we had the mountain location, aerial photos, and arm strength. Our team of 12 met and were briefed along the way.  We all knew what to do. We knew each others talents and  had a plan but even a plan is just a suggestion when push comes to shove. Rarely does the plan ever follow the same rules and that is why we have to know each other well so we can improvise when necessary. To our pleasant surprise everything was going along smoothly. We were able to reclaim the one we sought, along with two other bystanders. This is typically the case, to find others that have been kidnapped.  Only when it allows within the success of our mission do we bring them along. Sometimes it would hinder our mission of the one who is paying us, then we set them free, give them directions and food but that is it. Everything has to be on a strict time frame.

Success is the only option.

As we packed out for extraction some visitors arrived and all went on hold. Two covered trucks
with four armed guards. We waited until we could move or have to stand and overcome the new players. They looked around and seemed suspicious. Two kept watch while the other two began to unload the cargo. This is the norm for these camps to move and take patrol in this way. When the first two approached three of our guys they were taken out silently. This means we either move or finish the other two. If we can leave it is always best to fit the plan. First we must know their intent before we leave and determine if it would impede our success.

Three of us moved in to get a visual on the other two and what their cargo was, it never hurts to collect a little extra

cash if possible. We were in position. I was totally back to the self I needed to be to do this work. Then it happened. The two men were unloading 19 young girls from about kindergarten to high school. My mind froze for a second and that was not good. Not good because this meant they would be busy long enough for us to move out without needing to act on these two or their cargo. Before my experience with the human trafficking I would not have had another thought as my buddies were already on their way back to connect with the others to move on. I found my self in a place that I was not familiar with. Something was more important and I knew what was going on. My team mates were calling me in to leave and I could only look at them, then the kids, then back again. Then I made the call to stay as I motioned for my team to leave without me. The problem is that it does not work this way. It is all in or all out. It is a collective mind. I was in a battle with myself now. The direction of my future lay directly in front of me. This choice would determine my path.

One of my team mates moved to my location, call him Sam. Sam was Hispanic and blended well in this environment, one of the reasons he was selected for this mission. I could tell he was not happy because my hesitation was putting us all at risk. We could easily end the two that were left but that is not the rules til the rules change. Sam was really pissed and showed it.

"Z, what they hell", he yelled.

"They are kids, Sam", I yelled back.

"Grrrrrrrr", Sam growled at me.

"I know Sam, but I got to stay. Take everyone home and I will find my own way", I pleaded.

"It don't work that way and you know it man", he sternly reminded me.

"I know, I know! No grey areas! Just leave ME TO TAKE CARE OF THIS", I insisted.

"Hold on Z", said Sam and he disappeared into the chopper. When he returned with a few more of my team, I knew I had created a storm. Still, I was answering to a higher calling now. Now that I knew about human trafficking, held children for hours out of rescue, my cellular makeup had been changed for good.

I knew the team would be arguing now and I only had a few seconds. My attention drew away from the team as I heard screaming and crying from one of the huts the two had taken them. I knew there was a man at the truck with some of the girls in the cage. There was another man inside the hut where the screams were coming from. I moved and entered the hut without the others knowing. I found the one with his pants down had the youngest held by her hair. I ended his actions immediately. The girls screamed in fear of not knowing who I was or what would happen to them. I tried to quiet them to no avail. I knew the other would be coming so I prepared but nothing happened next, until Sam busted through the door!

Like old faithful he had come through for me! He had taken out the other so for the moment we were safe. Although the girls were frightened out of their minds. Sam was able to speak in their language witched calmed most of them down. Sam turned to me and said that they might try to escape out the door and to block it.

Sam said to me, "Z, you bastard, you stuck us between rocks. The team exited with the kidnapped. I stayed, along with Rocco and Lar. Please tell us what we are doing? Why are you putting death on our heads", he questioned angrily and confused.

Impatiently I answered, "I told you to leave me, let me be the causality, this is my war"!

Sam yelled back at me, "You don't have a war Z, you are one of us 'til it is over"!

So I instructed, "If that is true then help me get these kids to safety. Think of them as being on life support and help me act fast"! I whispered in his ear quickly what these kids were being used for and where they were going. The change in his facial expression proved he was understanding this new mission. He went to fill in Rocco and Lar as I stayed watch over the children. They looked so young and innocent as they hugged each other crying. The older ones looked at me angrily for a way to escape. When Sam returned he said the others were in but not happy about it. I reassured him that before this was done they would understand and be glad they stayed behind to help.

We got the girls out! Sam and Lar tried to explain to them that we were here to help but we needed their help also. The kids were not sure what to make of this and we had to determine witch ones were with us. Time was moving fast and we had to make our move. We loaded up all in one truck. We set out to find a church before anyone could see us. One of the girls told us where she thought she had seen a church. Many churches in these parts looked similar to any other hut to the untrained eye. We drove opposite from the girls directions and that caused a panic. We had to reassure them that we were merely avoiding being seen. We

explained that we were only there to get them to safety.
Then we would leave them on their own.
They referred to us as "Boss".

We had several problems in transit and were on the road for many hours. Lack of food was our biggest hurdle. Everything else was improvisation. We came near a house that was just off the road. We were unknowns and we would not be treated well by anyone and we knew this. We knew how to handle this and took action. I took Roc with me and approached the house. We asked if they were religious so not to tip our hat that we where looking for a church. They were very non compliant and we also expected this. We had to use force and we took most of their food leaving them some rice. We took some palm tarps to cover the truck with and made the husband lay on floor with a gun to his head. The wife and kids screamed! Roc secretly gave the wife a thousand dollars making them rich. We then took off but as we were leaving the wife ran to us and told us there was a church a short distance down the road and how to find it in the dark. Her husband came out and was pissed yelling at us. This is how it works, you as a local do not help anyone like us or you will be killed. So we took what they would have given us if we had been local so to save face. We paid them knowing they would tell on us but they would wait until
morning when it did not matter, because we would be long gone. It is a game that you learn after many times doing this.

We made it to the church as fast as possible. Our intention was to find the next church so to end the path that anyone chasing us would think we were no longer worth their time. There was no church for many days travel but there was a town about a 3 hour drive away. In this town was an orphanage that could help us. They had an underground

railroad to save these kids but we needed introduction. I asked the priest to come but he refused knowing he would already be in trouble if anyone found out we had talked to him. So there was only one other thing to do, and that was to have someone in his place to go with us. I saw a young nun behind one of the buildings and ask the priest about her. He said she was new and he would not allow anyone to go with us. I sent Sam to get her and bring her here. He did and she approached not very willing, resisting actually. The Priest protested. The young nun spoke English. We asked her to come, then the Priest interrupted and she shyed away. I grabbed her by the arm and took her to the truck. She fought me every step of the way until she saw the kids and halted. With out hesitation she got in the truck and said she would take us there. Spirit was moving swiftly through all of us.

We gave the priest money, he was happy as we left. As we approached the town the nun asked
to pull over and we did. She told us she would walk to town and talk to the orphanage then she would return. We agreed but we made sure that she explained it to the kids what she was doing. With that she left and after she was out of sight we moved closer to town and hid the truck in case she was deceiving us or if trouble followed her back. As time passed it seemed the kids were finally on our side but we kept an eye on them just the same. It also gave us time to strategize. Roc, Lar, and Sam confirmed they were all in. Before they were in because this is how a team works but now they were in because they believed it was the right call. They called me names and threw stuff at me for dragging them into this possible suicide mission. I already knew this was coming, it is how we handle things like this. It is like an extreme band of brotherhood. No matter what one of us do the others sink or swim with us. That is what keeps us alive.

The nun was taking a lot longer than expected and we were looking at new options now. Trying to determine if she had been taken or turned us in or could not find the help we needed. She did finally come back with three others. Her plan was to take a few of the kids back at a time with one of the people she had brought with her. She said this is what the lady of the underground told her to do. We knew this was not the way we were going to do it. Way too much risk and maybe these men she brought were with the bad guys and by the time we knew what happened they would be gone with the kids. So no, that is not the way it was going to happen. We explained we would drive next to town. We would drop a group off with each of these men along with one of ours and they would be far enough apart to not attract attention. Then each would find their own way to the orphanage. We gathered some clothes together we received from church donations. This helped to blend in. That is how we did it. One by one the groups arrived and were taken in from different entrances. Once inside I met with the lady in charge of the underground. She was not happy with my change of plans but understood once I explained it. She went into detail how she would handle this and it did not meet my approval. We agreed to spend the night. I had disposed of the truck at a distance from town and knew it would be discovered sooner or later but in the water it was not of much use.

I went back to the guys and explained that I did not think the lady liked us much. They all laughed and ask so what is next. I again gave each of them a way out. They had already broken
all the rules and committed to follow this to get the girls safe. This had been done to a point in my opinion that I could take it from here. There was no reason that they needed to take this to another level, that at this point it

would be taking a vastly different path. After seeing the extremes that these traders of flesh were willing to do I knew that there was no one yet I could trust except my guys and the nun. So now I told the guys to hang tight and I would go get the nun. I left the room and hunted for the nun and found her with the boss lady of the orphanage. I ask her to come with me and she did so but I could see on the boss ladies face she was not happy about this. My first impressions of her may have been right. The nun followed me back to where the guys were and I closed the door. Roc stood near the door to make sure we were secure. We all had our talents and this was one of his, always there all the time.

I addressed the nun first, "Mam, I thank you for helping us when you knew the risks. I believe you are one to be trusted. You have done all we ask and more. We have taken on the safety of these little girls and we don't take that lightly. We have found ourselves is a situation that we are not completely comfortable with, finding it hard to trust anyone. Since I have taken on the responsibility of these kids I have to do what I think is best so if anything goes wrong it is on me and me alone. At this time I am asking you if you trust me? I am giving you a choice to stay with us 'til I am satisfied with the children's safety or if you would like to go on your own way now"?

The nun looked around at the guys then back at me with tears in her eyes as she spoke, "Sir, I came because I knew I had to. I could feel God telling me to. I did not think we would make it this far".

"Why", we asked?

She explained that the priest was associated with the bad people who owned the children for business. Not because

he wanted to but because he is scared of them. So we asked if she was scared also.

Tears flowed from her eyes as she said yes, but she knew her life as a nun would not be safe or easy.

Her emotion was getting to all of us big strong tough guys. I asked if she wanted to stay with us all the way to seeing the girls to safety and she accepted. She said there was nothing more important that she could do with her time. We thanked her for trusting us and helping us.

She addressed me as "Sir", so I asked her to call me Z. She said very quietly, "Z, I don't trust the boss lady, I don't know why it is just a feeling".

I felt the same and this confirmed why we needed the nun to stay with us and help.

Lar spoke up now, "Z, I know I cussed at you for hours after you put us in this position. Every time a new twist comes along in this adventure, I begin to think. I have not thought of anything in sooo long, other than the shitty work we have to do. Now I don't know whether to shoot you or hug you. But guys, I don't think we will be welcome here much longer, we will need a plan".

The nun spoke up and asked what we planned to do? I answered that our first priority was to get them to a place of safety and into the hands of people that can love them and tend to their needs.
I asked the nun if she knew of people that could help us with this. The nun seemed to drop her head in prayer.

When she looked up she had a smile on her face and said, "In my travels from the sea, when I first got here, there

were families in towns where I served, that hid local people the government wanted to arrest. They were not bad people, no they were helping others that were starving and sick. Some were doctors and nurses from here and other countries that the government did not like because of their politics. At least that is how the government explained it, but these people had no politics that I could see. There were people that came to our churches to take them to a place where they were safe and these churches I study at were connected with these people. The priests would hide them 'til they could move them out with these people. It was like a big secret but I knew. Yes I knew, I see things you know but I don't dare say anything".

We wanted to know if she could take us to some of these people? How far would we have to travel? She explained that it would take many days journey by car. Sam pulled out a map from our earlier gig and she showed us the way. She went on to explain that it was not a safe journey even without the kids or her.

I said somewhat under my breath that we were going to need a plane. With that Lar got up and started for the door, exclaiming that he would find us a plane. Out the door he went! That was one of his talents, he could find anything anywhere, even a plane in the middle of the jungle.

We had awhile 'til it got dark so we could leave with the least amount of notice. We gathered supplies as we could find them and some food while the nun went back and kept the boss lady busy. When Lar got back he had located a helicopter. It was one of the old carrier types with plenty of room for all of us. Funny how some things work out, maybe an angel was with us.
Now we had to get there. We were looking at about an hour walk, maybe longer with the kids in tow. So the nun

needed to tell the kids what we were doing and that we needed to be quiet because we did not trust the people here. They all seemed to have gained trust in us now and that was very important. Some of the kids were used to these things, it is different in these lawless areas where it was a constant way of life to not know who was good and who was bad. Most everyone keeps to themselves. Then once it was time I got the nun and we all met with the kids. They were all ready and in the game. It amazes me how kids are so adaptable. We left the compound without much notice and it actually took less time than we had thought. We arrived at the airport with ample time to do what we needed.

We made it to our destination! The nun took us many places as we kept the kids in hiding in the open. As we continued to move we picked up people that the nun knew and were there to help us take care of these kids. There were also others that took some of the kids in to be part of their families. What amazed me was how we all came from the hate and evil that brought these kids to where they were when I first found them. Then to a progressing of standing up knowing that it would surely wreck the path that I was on. Not that it was a great path but you become comfortable with what is familiar. This is similar to these kids in the brothels, if there is only uncertainty in where the rescue takes them they many times return to the brothel.

One has to realize these kids only have a limited amount of experience to draw from. This is the easiest way to understand what is not understandable….. Now after layers of no trust we have been placed with a line of those who do not question our intent. They love these wonderful creations they receive from us, guide us to food and places to stay. With each step we are being educated. Some of us finding our place in this world. The Nun walks with

incredible effort. Something inside made her continue. Now we can all see that she has become our boss. My team stood with me because I was their team mate. Now they too have become different in their evolution of this life's path. Like the nun, I walked with effort 'til something inside of me took over and I followed. Here we are rediscovering a new definition of the old Underground Railroad.

We were far removed from the geographical location where this all started. We crossed over many gorilla fighting units' territories, so this puts us in a neutral state of awareness. We can work freely now and establish reality for what we have left to do. The nun talked to several priests along our journey trying to establish the ones that were truthful. The nun impressed all of us with her methods of interrogation. You know many of us know what it is like to hit the bottom, maybe not like these kids but you get the idea. When we hit this bottom we have many friends or so we thought 'til that day really comes. You reach out and don't find any hands. Anger fills you 'til it gets in your way and eating becomes the most dominate thought. You realize that when push comes to shove not many are really willing to interrupt their lives to accommodate the broken one. Words don't always translate into action. You can't really blame them because they did not put you here. Then you find you are on your own. At this time you decide to accept your fate or to fight and see what will come. These kids don't have the tools to find the fight, only in the beginning is fight a thought. Then as time progresses they conform to their new surroundings and masters. Yet some have something that cannot be described that this fight may go dormant for a while but when the opportunity arises they act. Even if they succeed each step requires another set of tools whether it be something they have learned or seen. Maybe it's something inherent within them.

This is why this quest we are walking through right now is so important to us. We do not merely rescue the kids. We do all we can to release them in a place where they have the opportunity to advance to the next evolution of their humanity. When you have allowed yourself to be compassion and unconditional love, you really don't need to think anymore you just know what is right and what is wrong. In this moment in our path we have given our souls to the rescue of these kids. If it demands our life or anything else we will without thought. When one signs this contract with oneself they become a very dangerous force to the evil. When two in the same space commits to this it becomes twice as dangerous to the evil they face. In our situation we had 5 then with each connection we met there was another and another. I pity any one that gets in our way from this point forward.

With four kids left in our care we started to develop a sort of relationship. We really did not need a language anymore unless it was just having fun. The girls trusted us and would do anything we told them. They saw what was happening and were more than willing to comply. They had fun with each other and were well fed. With less need for protection, they stayed well within our sight. Also we gathered some people that journeyed with us. It really felt so good to know what I have learned about this crime against humanity. To see these kids when it was the end for them, to what they are becoming now. To see eyes clear, a smile form, go from filthy to clean and taken care of. It feeds the missing parts of my heart. As I watch them I feel a hand on my shoulder. It is Sam. I turn to look him in the eyes. He is a bit shorter than me and his eyes look up at mine. They begin to tear up as he attempts to speak, but nothing comes out. He gathers himself and tries again. He wants me to tell him this is all a nightmare that he will wake up from soon. But of course I can not do that.

I say, "Sam it is how it is".

Then like an unhappy adolescent he says, "No, I don't want it".

So I ask, "What is it you don't want"?

"For this to be a reality in our world.  I hate you for this, you brought me here. You are supposed
to be my friend you bastard", he exclaimed. I let him vent because when I first faced this I was alone. I had no one to direct my anger at or anything, I just had to eat it and see what happened.
Sam was ready to speak again, "Man, I should not have said that. I am sorry, Z".

To lighten the mood I playfully called him a crybaby sissy. Then I got serious and said, "Because of choices we have made we have found this on our path. It was inevitable, you know".

"What", asked Sam?

So I went on to explain, "We have learned talents and we chose this path of a mercenary to get rid of some of that anger we have for life and people. We use it as an excuse to do bad things to bad people so we will not have guilt. Somehow we forgive ourselves because we are righting the wrongs of this world for zero praise or glory but for pay. Our denial of what would happen on this journey is removed by the moment that we have to live in. We are all afraid to have that time to breathe and think because something like this could happen. I breathed a short time ago but did not give it much because I still did not want to see clearly. The problem is that I did see, when this started

to happen with the kids. I knew it before I saw what was going on. I cracked from the moment to the reality and I breathed again. This time it was too late for me because I already made the decision to act in hopes I could become human again. It just so happens that I let you breathe too".

Sarcastically he said, "So can I blame you suckah"!

So I answered, "If you need to buddy, if it makes you feel better".

"What do we do after all this", Sam questioned.

I had no answer for that question.

"You know Z, I really don't care what happens now. I am free, I'm free", he yelled! Then he spun around and chased the girls. He picked them up and spun them too until they all fell down laughing.

When the nun returns, she gathers us to brief us on her findings. I can tell that Roc and Lar are in the same state as Sam and that is good to know. The nun tells us she did not get any straight answers but she knows where the kids need to go. She tells us that at first she just thought they did not want to be involved and that they would always suggest an orphanage. At first I thought they were just trying to get rid of me but then something came to me. These Priests really did not know well the other Priests but they were in the same community. Yet I found out that some of the Priests did know each other but would not admit to it... These priests all recommended the same orphanages, not like the others but two specific ones. After leaving them I also noticed they were trying to lead me to these places without saying it. I think a bell went off in my head. (Everyone

laughed, she was so serious). "So I think we should take them there?"

I touched the nun's hand, looked at her and asked, "Why do you want to take them there"?

Her reply was, "Because that is where they need to go. I am sure of this place Z".

"OK", I say, "but we are not going to just waltz in and introduce ourselves. I think that if everyone agrees then we go to the closest one and sit up outside of town and let the nun go in and check it out". Everyone nods and says yes. We have an agreement. I look at the Nun, still holding her hand. I say to her, "We will tell you what you need to ask and how to ask it before we make any decisions. Are you ok with this"?

"Yes", she answered with courage in her heart!

We set off the next day. It was a three day journey by private transportation from a relative of one of the police the nun met through a Priest. Phew! It was a long, slow and hard journey but we made it! We walked into town at nightfall. We found accommodations and we talked through the night practicing with the Nun how to ask questions and what we needed to know. Then we rehearsed anything we thought might be asked. Once we thought we had prepared her for anything we all slept for a few hours. Then the Nun headed off to visit the Orphanage. Several hours passed until we all started to become worried. We knew that the Nun liked to talk and so did all the people in this region. Then just as we were going to set out after her she walked in. She faced the door not letting us see her face for a moment then she turned. There was a smile on her face that we had not seen since we met her. She was very happy. She

had confirmed they did help kids that had been abused, sold, tortured and trafficked. They had a special way to bring them back into what would help them deal with all they have been through and teach them what life should be like. They then let them decide what they want to be, and help them be that. They council them with professionals that volunteer and they keep their past hidden if they want. When they leave the orphanage they have skills to help them have an advantage over other people. So far all that have passed through this place have been successful in their lives. They did know the Priests I had talked with and they even knew I was coming. The location and operation are kept secret because they feel it needs to be kept that way for the safety of the kids and volunteers.

Our job was over. We all knew it, except the nun, she had a new job and she would be great at it. She knew she found it and you could see the happiness in her face even when she was yelling at someone. It was rather comical and at same time practical. I decided to stay for a month and help fix things that were broken. My team also could have left but for some reason stayed as long as me. Lar stayed even longer. We all bought supplies that the Orphanage needed. Sam bought so many toys it was fun to watch. This was a really odd adventure for us. I was blessed to see how so many people were changed by all these little girls. I don't think anyone really understood how this all came to be but I think we all are satisfied with the outcome. On the plane ride home all I could wonder was why was I going home? What would all this mean in my future? I guess that feeling inside will tell me the answers and I will be there to respond.

# Chapter 8

## Working for a Brothel owner

As a bounty hunter I became skilled in capturing my prey.

I found success in becoming the one I hunted.

I lived in the same neighborhoods.

I made the same friends.

I frequented the same places.

I selected out the worst of the worst.

If I was going to do this work, I would go in deep and make a difference.

I could get pulled into a depth of subtle amnesia of the soul/self.

I lost my two partners to violence perpetrated by who some would consider petty criminals.

Never underestimate the varying degrees of criminal out there.

All can be dangerous in certain circumstances.

After years of this, I lost my will to live.

Denied by spirit was my attempt to end it.

I hoped I would not reach that point again in this new learning experience.

I would become the protector of the brothel owner.

This would challenge me to the core.

I would be sought out by this Man for my talents.

I would be in high demand for my services.

I would know the inside information.

I would learn more about this virus infecting our world.

I would go further into the catacombs of this business of kids for sale.

I would be effective in this passion to end human trafficking.

Like graduating from school and applying all you know.

No more time for thoughts and books, time for action.

Risk it all.

Something beyond words drove me to know, so I could do what had now become me.

Save children, feed the poor and give help to the sick and dying.

Bringing hope to the hopeless became my obsession.

In most of my life I felt something was guiding my footsteps along the path.

I often hear people talk about subjects that claim to be an authority.

They can only claim this based on what they have heard or read about the subject.

People accept what touches their heart.

No matter if it is true or not.

Some never think to find the truth for themselves.

If I was to do this I had to know for my self first hand what the truth was and why.

My goal is to make a difference, not to make money or feed ego.

I live to utilize this knowledge to save the enslaved children of this earth.

During my free time, I made a commitment not to lose myself internally by what I became externally. I chose Cambodia because it was common place here. I could work anonymously. I could now walk the streets with out being seen, thus finding those who were up to no good. My goal was to mix in with them, gain their respect, and then take it to the next level. Not as one of them, but as one they

feared. I would mingle with the dirty police force and there I would do the same. I would show enough vulnerability to let them in and feign control over me. This would put me in a position for those I sought, (brothel owners) to want me as their security.

I walked around one night and observed the usual men gambling on the corner.

I asked to join.

To which they stared blankly at me until I pulled out a wad of cash.

Game on!

Now I was the new best friend.

They played a common game and this gave me time to observe the crowd for friend and foe.

As I suspected I found them cheating. I kept quiet until I noticed a man who stood out from the others. I could see him glare at the dealer each time he lost. The customer was in pretty deep and visibly annoyed. The dealer showed some fear of this man and arranged for him to win a few rounds. I felt my timing was right so I called the dealer out on his cheating. I knew this would attract the attention of the others to protect him.

Guns drawn as I expected.

I also had a good hunch that the serious customer would weigh in on this matter. I needed to show authority with the security. I could only hope my play would be assisted by this serious customer stepping in so I would not be

screwed. I quickly disarmed the two men and without haste was able to bend the dealer down over the table. I acted like I was about to cut off his arm for cheating. Just then the serious man stepped up to intervene!

He gracefully reached for my shoulder and whispered for me to back down. He said in my ear that he would take care of this with benefit for us both. I looked him directly in the eyes, with arms and fists clenched tight. We all slowly and with caution backed away. I was sure to keep my back to the wall, eyes open for impending threats. I looked again at the serious man who tipped his hat and said to wait for his friend to arrive. The air around us grew thick like fog and heavy like ice. By this time most others had scattered who did not want to be involved in the matter at hand. Fear filled everyone's eyes, wondering what would happen next. Moments later, a big round man arrived on scene. He greeted the serious man and they appeared to be buddies.

They chatted privately for a few minutes then invited me over to where they stood. The serious man introduced himself to me by the name of Jam. He reassured me that we would be treated to a wonderful time and that our losses would be replaced with much more. He introduced the other man as Nha, and said he was the owner of the property that we were on. Jam explained that they were old friends, but the dealer was unaware of this, and would be dealt with accordingly. He saw my approval and took the opportunity to place his hand on my shoulder and show interest.
He said he wanted to get to know me more. I was invited to Nha's for a drink and conversation.

I accepted the invitation with my heart racing.

I hoped this would get me what I wanted: RESPECT IN THE UNDERWORLD.

We traveled by private car and driver outside the city just after sunset.
It was like something from a movie: tall walls, armed guards, and an enormous home.
I was now fully committed to this cause.
I prayed and hoped I had not just passed the line of no return for the night.

All though somewhat casual, we sat in a large room filled with abundance and riches.
Whiskey was served by a man who then took his place against the wall. Attractive ladies entered for the sole purpose of giving attention to Nha and making Jam feel special too. When two more came in for me, I looked away and turned all my attention and focus on the men. They laughed and told me to relax and enjoy the moment. They said the past was in the past. I showed a little relaxation while keeping my focus.

Jam turned to me and took a breath before he entered a dialogue with me, "My friend, I don't know your name".

"Dog", I replied.

"Really, that does not seem like a nice name to be called", he said somewhat suspiciously. I did not respond. "Ha maybe it fits, in a good way", he smoothed things over.

I had to play the game so I could be the one with authority here. So I stood up and addressed them, "Thank you for your time but I need to leave, you mentioned you would return my money".

Jam stood. I could see he was not used to this. He looked at Nha and back at me. "My friend, no need to leave we want to know who you are", he persuaded.

"Why", I questioned matter of factly..

"I assure you Dog, it is for mutual benefit. I will not waste your time", Jam says.

My play had worked. This put us on equal ground now. I looked at Nha who was smiling. He motioned for me to sit down so I complied.

Jam appeared to be a bit more at ease now as he leaned over to compliment me, "Dog, you sure handled yourself well back there, on all levels. I know, I was watching you".

"And…. So…." I question bluntly.

"We are business men. We keep a look out for people who can help us keep out businesses safe", he explained.

"Maybe you should get the police to help you", I say rather casually.

They both chuckled and explained plainly that yes, they do own them but the work they do is like shit.

"Well I don't work for anyone", I blurted out.

They reassured me that I "would not need to work for them but WITH them instead".

So I enlightened them, "I don't do partnerships either"!

They looked at each other baffled, asking if there could be another way. Then they uttered the words, "Contract work". Now they were speaking my language so to speak. I was regaining my confidence. Everyone smiled and felt more at ease. Jam ordered more drinks and the girls increased in "friendliness". I noticed the men standing guard around the walls stand down a little. This told me that they were not professionals and did not have the training I had. I observed two open doors in the room to my advantage. I let things unfold as they may and held my position. I would get what I came here for then I would exit this country with haste.

Nha spoke now with a bit of superiority, "Dog, we run several businesses here in town. We need an overseer. It is always questionable whether we are getting all the money we make. Also, there
are competitors seeking to take our business".

"What would you like me to do", I ask, getting to the point.

Jam stepped in and took over the conversation, "Well Dog it is like this, we lack a manager to keep an eye on what is going on in each of these businesses. The ones we had have had, say unfortunate accidents or disappeared".

"And why is that", I question.

"We have our suspicions, which got us nowhere" they said. We thought it was one of the boys from China or Russia, but they would have forced the issue by now if that were true".

So I spoke up and said, "To me it sounds like you have someone within your organization that has created a business within and has some of your people working for him. That would explain why your people keep coming up

missing. I can take care of this for you but you need to give me free reign".

Jam looks at Nha and then looks back at me and says that could be a problem. So we sit in silence for a few minutes while the wheels of the mind were turning. So my comeback to their comment was, "Maybe then, what ever they are stealing from you is the cost of doing business".

"If we let you in, you could become that person and then we would be working for you Dog", he said sternly.

I scoffed at them, stating, "I am on contract. This is what I do. I don't want your business or to be a boss. I want to solve your problem, get paid and move on". Both Jam and Nha looked at each other and nodded affirmatively. So I went on, "I will take care of this problem and you will pay me $30,000 USD and we will both be happy"!

There was a pause, then Jam spoke first, "That is far too much money my friend, we are but mere business men".

I looked at Nha for his response and he got a big smile on his face. I asked him what he thought, "So Nha, do you believe a weeks worth of your trade is worth liberating a few thieves in your company"? Jam looked at Nha and then back at me. As he turned to face me he handled the girl that was sitting on the arm of the chair in a sexual manner. This was a sign that the deal had just been made.

"So Dog when would you like to start this project", they asked with out hesitation.

I looked at the floor as though I was thinking but I already knew how it would work for me. I spoke up and said, "I need a guide to show me all around and introduce me as the

new partner and head of operations. I need to see all the books. I will need both of you to stay clear of me and limit your normal visits to the businesses".

I knew I would be limited from everything so I needed someone who knew all in order to find out what I needed. The person they would make my tour guide would do what they told him but I could use him to talk to the people I needed to get the info I wanted. I also knew I could easily solve their problem to get what I wanted from the beginning. This is how things work. I also needed to show them I was not a cop. That would have to present it self.

"Mr. Dog are you assassin", they asked in broken English.

I answered frankly, "I have many talents but there are those I do not choose to do".

Then they turned up the intimidation factor by stating that, "Just so you know, if you do anything more than what you hired for, we know many assassins".

I bowed in false respect as I kept a chuckle to my self. I gave off an air of seriousness as I thought inside that they may be powerful in their world but not in mine. Still I knew not to underestimate them, as our egos were currently residing in their world. They may own the town but they also had someone working within their world stealing from them. I looked up and assured them I was here to do my thing and they would not be there to say goodbye.

Everyone appeared to be happy. Jam and Nha looked at each other and laughed loudly. We all drank to the new found agreement.

I stood again and asked for my money from the earlier night's event. They laughed again. Nha motioned to one of the men from the wall.  He came and gave me my money. Jam stood also and spoke, "Dog, tomorrow night you will meet our guide as you say. Here where we met tonight. He will know who you are and will be at your call 24/7. He will bring you half your money and you will get the rest on completion".

I chime in with, "You will pay me the rest just before we conclude, to avoid any tearful goodbyes". They chuckled again and said they liked "Mr. Dog".

With that I was on my way out. One of the men was prepared to give me a ride any where I needed to go. Then I had an idea so I turned back at the door and said, "Hey partner,
I will need to take that Lexus over there for my cover".

Jam motioned his men to throw me the keys and I was off!

I drove to the next town and found an ok hotel and checked in. I got two rooms so I could move between them for security. I would do business in one and make it known that is where I stayed and keep the other one where I actually stayed. So it begins, I really did not expect things to move so quickly. It makes me wonder if I had help from the other side. In any case I saw the opportunity and took it. I expect that in the next few days I would be treated like a celebrity if they actually do spread the word that I am the new partner. This will make it so I don't need to hunt as hard for what I am looking for. Most of what I will do will depend on my tour guide. The only problem I see is staying in control of my emotions regarding what I am about to learn. I went into this knowing I cannot change anything, that would serve nothing, but what I learn about the trafficking

of little kids will then be my opportunity to make a difference in more than one place with more than one child. How I will react to what I see will be the most difficult part. I cannot be involved if I am to be successful. We will see, lord I pray I will not lose myself.

I woke early in the morning and got my act together. I waited on a phone call to start work but did not get one. So I checked out my neighborhood and got comfortable with the area. I needed to look like I have been here before and this was not my first go around. I knew most of this work would be done at night and took a nap. After a few hours of rest I gathered my gear and headed out the door to go to the make shift casino. I got a call from Tico who would be my guide in this new business I was a part of now. To his surprise I was just around the corner. He seemed a little intimidated by me. I gathered this to be that he was not really the one in charge that was suppose to be assigned to me. I let it ride a little while and he obviously was not who I needed to be my tour guide of the business. So I told him to have his bosses call me when they were serious. I left him at that moment and went back to my hotel. I clicked on the TV and had a beer. It was not long before Jam called me on the phone.

"Dog what is going on", he demanded.

"Not much Jam", I said calmly.

"Why you not working Dog", he commanded?

So I fired back, "You told me you would send me a boss to show me around and open all the doors. I told you without that the chance of success is not very good. We had deal and now I don't like much Jam. I think you are playing me"!

He came back with, "Hold on Dog, we don't know you! We needed to see who you were before we open big door. If you are not who you claim to be things would get very dark for both of us. We would win in the end but why go through that"?

I did not respond.

"Dog", he exclaimed.

"What", I answered!

"You with me", he questioned.

"Still thinking about it", I answered.

"Let me ask you, how did you know the guy we sent was not the guy you wanted", Jam inquired?

"Because I am who I told you I was. Now, let me ask you a question…" I asked Jam.

"Sure", he answered.

"Why should I not kill you now", I asked emotionless.

There was a long and silent pause on the other end of the line.

I spoke again, "You still there Jam? Let me tell you; I left your person at the casino and came home to have a beer and decide what to do with you and your friend. Then you called me. Look, I don't think you have ever met anyone like me and you have gotten in deep with your businesses. So I will give you a break. I know you need me. You could

lose everything you have built up to this point. I have seen that many times by people like you in many places. If you don't know the truth I am speaking to you right now then we need to go our separate ways"…I waited to listen to see if he was hearing me….he was listening so I went on, "If you are going to play this game and make a deal with someone like me you must know the terms and understand the consequences. I am not here to take your business, I don't want to do your work, I want to do the job we agreed to and move on. You pay me for this and each of our lives are better. Then we both have someone to call on in the future. Do you hear me Jam"?

"Yes sir, ah Dog", he said.

"Good answer, let's forget this mishap and start fresh tomorrow. Jam you do understand we will not be talking like this again correct" I ordered.

"Yes", said Jam.

"Ok, tomorrow night I will call you with my location. You send me your manager who knows everything and can unlock all doors" I said.

"Yes", was his final word.

I hung up the phone, finished my beer and fell asleep watching a movie. This was good news and I was very lucky to find myself in this position. This is not unusual that these scum bags have not a clue of what they are into. It is small town and just by circumstances they find themselves in a position of authority. They know everyone and everyone knows them. They just happen to be the ones to capitalize on this situation. One thing leads to the next and they are these guys. These countries are mostly lawless

and not overseen buy the larger government and they virtually become the government. I was hoping for this and as luck have it that is what I found. I knew going into this I would either be dead or running, or in the exact position I am now. It is a bit of an oxymoron that I say lucky. Jam and Nha are like little kids running the candy store full of ego and I will use this. I have a feeling that the ones stealing from them are a bit smarter and will take the business from them if I don't do anything. I will decide later how I use this for the future beyond what I came here to learn.

The next night I did what I said and gave Jam the place to have his manager meet me. I was not there so I could see if I had been set up. I see the manager arrive and look for me. It was not that hard to figure out who he was. These guys are amateurs. That is good for me. I sneak up on him. I lead him a few blocks away to a bar where we can talk. I take control of the situation until I feel comfortable with him and what we are doing. After awhile of talking I can determine this guy is legit. He opens many conversations about the businesses and offers to take me to them. He is under the assumption that I am Jam and Nha's partner and will be very active in the business. He also tells me all the books of each business are open for me all I have to do is ask and he will deliver. Now I have a place to start. The reason I am here. This is what I needed to get where I wanted.

The businesses are basically everything in this town, all the way to the police. Yes the police are also a business. I have my new friend Cam give me a tour of the town as I scope out exits if needed. He introduces me to everyone that has any significance. One officer, just under the Chief, showed me a warm welcome.

The thing most people won't understand is that this isn't seen as corrupt.

The businesses, the Police, the governments…

This is how it has been done a long time.

The kids used this way are also considered normal.

A girl is a burden unless she can be used in some way.

So it is the culture.

Though changing in time it remains prevalent and persistent in existing in many third world countries.

This makes it ever the more difficult for folks in the rest of the world to comprehend.

It becomes complicated for a human like me who walks the line between spirit and physical.

It you consider what I said you will see it is not a leisure path to walk.
Spirit guides the moral compass. That is undeniable to anyone.
However, life's norms are accepted differently everywhere you go.
Do you start a war that you cannot win?
Or do you create events that will someday win the war?
I create events and save lives, one at a time along the way.

Over the next week I grew familiar with all of the businesses. I figured out who was stealing. I would put that on hold while I created a map. Then I could get to where I needed to be in this. The majority of the revenues came

from the brothels so I led Cam to believe that was the area of my focus. What was unique is that the brothels are all home grown here and no outside influence has forced a take over from gangs such as the Chinese or Ukraine but that is just a matter of time. I told Cam this and he believed everything I told him and was willing to help in anyway he could to keep this in the family so to speak. He knew his salary was dependent on this business. Now with this I could work freely in knowing this business from beginning to end.

Over the following days I managed to pull off carte blanche alone time in all the brothels.

Everyone knew of me and let me come and go as I pleased. All were trying to make a good impression on me since they thought I was one of the owners. This got harder and harder for me each time I saw the little girls doing what they do in these places and not being able to do anything about it. I had to keep my mind focused and know what I witnessed would help the many rather than the one.

I became what I was expected to be, a partner in this business. I did not like it but it was what it was. I arranged with Cam to meet the next day and go deeper now that my story was accepted.

The conditions in these brothels are hard to describe. Let's say you leave crumbs, some trash, dirt, bugs and roaches and you are on your way to understanding what the girls rooms were like. There was little food to go around and the girls actually had to ask to eat. These kids were treated less than animals.

There were five locations in town and seven outside of town.

This I could do something about but not a lot. I explained to the managers that the kids could make more money and cost less for medicine if they were fed more. So they began to give them rice each day. At least it was something.

When I could I made records of all the kids and some of their names and descriptions for later use. Sometimes there would be more girls and sometimes less. I started to inquire where the kids would go or come from and I was met with some resistance. I explained that I did not see this operation to be effective economically and wanted to make it more efficient. This relaxed them to a point but I was still not getting the information I wanted. I took Cam outside away from the brothel. I told him with a mean attitude that something was going on here and I was not being told the truth! Cam did not look at me the entire time, he stared at the ground. He was shaking and I grabbed him by the arm and told him he needed to tell me right away. Cam then started to spill the beans and talked so fast I could not understand. I stopped him and told him this was his job and he needed to tell me what I wanted to know, I would not fire him unless he was stealing. I would make it so he would have the power over these guys.

Cam shook it off and said, "YES SIR"!

Cam told me they hired people they knew to buy the girls or kidnap them.

The kids were being bought from relatives for as little as $10-20 USD.

The guys would then sell them to the managers of the brothels.

This way everyone made a piece of the pie.

Both coming and going.

"Cam what you mean coming AND going" I asked?

"I mean, when they are finished and sold to the other managers" he answered.

"I still don't understand the finished part" I said.

Cam paused and I could see he was not comfortable with this part.

"Come on Cam you got to tell me" I urged.

"Well, you know you told the managers to feed them more", said Cam.

"Yes", I replied.

"Well, they don't want to feed them more because they will not get sick as fast" he explained.

Now I paused. I was having a hard time understanding this.

I looked at Cam and then looked at the brothel door.

"Cam why do they want the girls to get sick?" I dared ask.

Cam grabbed my arm. His already blood shot eyes filled with tears.

"They sell them for their body parts" he finally declared!

Cam looked away and covered his head.

I felt sick inside my own body.

Rage exploded inside me and a war for control began.

I could not expose myself no matter how this twisted me.

I looked at Cam still covering his head in disapproval and shame.

Although he did not like this, it is the way it is done in these places.

"Cam, I get it now, I understand you do not like this and I also understand that this is dark. I will not get you in trouble. You and I will work this out together", I said.

Cam nodded his head in relief.

As I looked away, I felt the war inside me grow. I wanted to do things that would make me as evil as they were. Or would it? All I could see in my head was killing these bastards in a hundred different ways. This part of the trafficking was like a business outside of the business. So what do I do with it, is the question. I looked over at Cam who still would not look at me. So I told him not to worry I will see him in a couple of days and all will be well. With that I head back to my hotel and had little thought of my security. I am stepping in deep now and when you mess with people's money you need to take warning. I have not stepped too deep but I did enough to cause trouble with feeding the kids more. So I had to make a plan how to work this now. I believe Cam will follow my lead and not go south on me, at least yet. He will wait to see what I do in the next couple of days. I needed to find out where these kids go to get cut up. I needed to know the doctors and the

transportation routes for where the organs go after they are harvested. This information would not be easy to get and would be on their time schedule. This gets sicker and sicker and I need to be someone else to deal with it emotionally. I don't know if I am ready for it but I don't have a choice now.

I think of the ocean and sitting on a beach somewhere by myself. It is not long and I am asleep. There is a noise that wakes me and I look at the clock, I've been asleep one hour. Without thought I have my gun in hand and finger on the trigger. I hear the noise again and it is a knock at the door. It seems persistent. It is from the room that I rented as my fake room so I make my
way through the adjoining doors. I closed quietly the door between the two rooms as I went. I am
grateful to have these two connecting units. I ask who is it and it is Cam. I open the door part way to keep my body out of the way. All I see is Cam. As I open the door more I see no one in the hallway. The coast is clear.

"Cam, you alone?" I ask.

"Yes", he confirms.

"What the hell you doing here, why are you not sleeping", I scowled.

"Boss, I have to talk to you", Cam said earnestly.
I let him in. I offer him a seat and a beer. This should be interesting.
He does not answer me and really looks shook up. I get him one anyway. He takes but doesn't drink it. Still looking at the floor he tries to start his story, "Boss promise me you will not kill me"!

"That depends, what did you do", I said.

"Nothing really, my wife and I well we just joined a church", said Cam.

"Why would I kill you for joining a church Cam", I asked, very confused by his stammering.

"Because I can't work for you anymore. What I have been learning has made me think about what I am doing", he said.

"It could not have been just the church Cam, you must have had this on your mind for awhile", I questioned.

"Yes, but it was the church that made me think about what I had been doing, then you make me go into the part I cannot live with. I thought I could just ignore some of what I do and go on. I have to support my family", he justified.

Cam begins to cry and is sweating a lot. I let him vent awhile to get it out. This gives me time to think about how I want to handle this. I have to look at it in many ways so I am not being played. I could tell from the start that Cam was not into this, there was something off. At first I thought he was evaluating me, but the further we went the more nervous he got. This could work even better than I thought if I play this right.

"Cam, I can not let you quit yet. I am sorry", I say.

He looks up at me and continues to whimper again.I put my hand on his shoulder and tell him it will be ok. He would need to trust me and help me get what I want. Then I would set him up where ever he wanted to go with his family. He would not have to worry about doing anything he did not

want to. His family would be proud of him and he would have time to forgive himself.

Cam looked up and stopped crying, "I don't understand Boss".

"You don't have to. I will not tell you until it is over. I need your knowledge", I said.

"Yes Boss", he said.

"Cam have you seen the teachings in your bible yet about how you will be challenged to measure your will and commitment to your faith", I asked him.

"No Boss", he answered.

"What I will ask you to do now is much greater than it was before. I will take you to the darkest place that haunts you. You will hate me for it. You will see what your actions have caused and the pain you have given so many. In the end you will hate yourself. Yet I will be there for you reminding you of your family and how they need you and you will then be able to start your new life", I explained.

"Boss", he questioned.

I talked over him, "You see Cam, when you make that decision to change and you ask for forgiveness that comes with a price. Many ask for it and do not really mean it. They think they do but most when challenged fall back and are weak. Let me ask you Cam, how much do you want what you told me?

"It is means everything. That is why I came here to tell you. I did not run. I expected you would have had me killed. I

want to leave with my family, If you did not kill me. I could escape with my family and travel far away to start again", he pleaded.

"Well Cam if you do what I ask of you and do not question it, I will not kill you. We will work swiftly; it cannot take long to accomplish this. You have to trust me and go in deep with me for a short time. Can you do this Cam? If not tell me now", I said.

"My family will be OK", he questioned.

"That is the deal and you will be OK also", I confirmed.

"I have many questions Boss", he lamented.

"Sorry that is not allowed. All your questions will be answered when it is over. Then you will not have to ask them", I said. "Cam how much do you know about what happens to the kids when the brothel is done with them"?

Cam looks up with tearful eyes watering again and takes a few short breaths, "Boss …,
I ….Know…. Everything"!

He in is in full on breakdown now and falls to his knees. He looks up at me and for the first time looks directly into my eyes.

"I know …
 names, businesses, doctors, aunties, families, houses, everything sir", Cam sobbed and exclaimed.

I sit on the floor with him and the pain flows to me now.

I have to keep the strength and push out the thoughts of the details that I imagine he knows.

"Cam, are you sure you can handle this? If you can't you will be of no use to me", I said.

"Sir, Dog, I believe you, I really do. I give my life to you to fulfill your promise. I know God will give me the strength. But for now I have to feel this", said Cam.

Cam is broken right now and I know that to be a good thing. Now I can use this to strengthen him. I thought maybe I did not come here to just save the kids and me but to save the lost ones on the way also. I think of the words I have heard many times before, Heaven will not give you anymore than you can handle. I pass these words on to Cam.

"Cam, I have a serious question for you now", I say.

Cam has recovered a little but still heavy on the floor.

"Yes Boss", he mutters.

"Why did you leave Buddhism for God", I question.

"I did not, I am just Christian now", he answers.

I chuckle and he also begins to laugh. Some will understand this question but also most will not. Just know it is the correct answer.

Cam manages to get to his feet. As he does he downs the can of beer I gave him. I grab his arm and lead him to the door. I talk softly to him before I open it and tell him nothing has changed and this night never happened. I told

him that his reward will be in every step he takes from this moment forward. Cam sort of smiles as he looks at the door and I open it and check the hall way as he leaves.

I go to the window and see him walking down the street without anyone near him. I think to myself, I just found a warrior. I intuit he was sent to me from somewhere other than here on this earth. I will not take lightly the gift. This also strengthens me in what I am here to accomplish. As hard as it gets to watch all these events go by without interfering will still be the toughest thing I will ever do. I see the gift of doing more than I could have imagined without his knowledge.

# Chapter 9

## Working in a Brothel part 2

The time has come to walk where few have ever roamed. Although dreading this reality, I accepted it and took the first step. Now is the beginning of the end of this part of my life. My mantra has been to get me through this with minimal sacrifice. I meet up with Cam and go over the plan. I look him in the eyes and stare to see if he is strong today. He smiles and says he is in! We trust each other now. We begin the walk, that makes the words, "thou I walk through the valley of the shadow of death", become real. As we get breakfast at a local restaurant it seemed locals were getting to know me as partners of the big guys. I didn't know if that was bad or good but I could work with it.

We went down the street across from our bigger brothel which held 60 kids inside. This is one of our prime locations. It is located near the large hotels which house and attract many foreigners. Cam takes me to a café near this brothel. Not sure of what his plan is but I will let it develop. We order some coffee, sit and watch. Some people that pass by acknowledge Cam and sometimes he introduces me. After 45 minutes I ask Cam what we are doing.

"Dog, you want to know the other side of this business? I know that some of the girls are about to be turned out. Some sick and no use anymore. This is the business in a

business you call it. I am not part of it, even though we all know about it. The manager is a really dark man. I think if we sit here that soon we will see the process begin", he explained to me.

"Ok, how long might we have to wait?" I questioned.

"No more than three days. We must wait for the Doctor to open for business." he said.

"Doctor?" I inquire.

"Yes, most of the transactions take place through him or another doctor because they make the most money this way from the girl. Sometimes they will sell the girl to a foreigner then I don't know what happens to her. I can only guess and I don't want to do that", he said timidly.

"Cam, we do have to know", I reminded him.

"Okay, okay, you keep reminding me", he said, giving in.

Three hours later, we see the dark man taking two girls out the door. Both look very sick, weak, and dirty. He passes them to one of the motorcycle taxis. Cam grabs my arm and says it's time to go. I tell him hold on and let them go, we know where they are going. Cam sits down and we wait until they are gone and the dark man goes back inside. Then we leave and make our way to the doctor.

"It is not a normal office", Cam tells me, "this is an office he hides behind his house for special patients".

We watch from across the street at a small store. My thoughts swirl now like a superhighway of the mind. I can see what is going on clearly. I feel like I do when working

as a soldier. I am feeling the horror of what has happened and is about to happen again. The war inside of me is taking me off my game so I breathe to get centered. Cam and I try to figure out when to make a move. We are rather lost at the lack of security. It seems as though the Doctor is alone with the kids but there could also be others inside. We are sure there is at least a nurse. We are going to need to get a closer look without attracting attention.

After weighing all our options we can only find one, which is to go directly to the front door. We go there and a lady or nurse answers. She looks a little nervous seeing us. Cam tells her we want to see the doctor and she explains that he is busy. I reach to the door and push it open. I explain to her who I am and she knows this already. Word travels fast. So at this point we have invited ourselves in so she gets the doctor. He appears to have been getting ready for the operation if you can call it that. I explain that I am checking all parts of our business. He does not know that this is part of my business. He really does not know how to deal with me and grabs his phone. Cam looks at me, I signal to stop him and he does.

"Look doctor I understand what you do and I need a little information from you. After that you will be able to go on with your business", I say.

"I don't know what you want and I don't work for you", he barks back.

I look at Cam, who responds, "Doctor, you do work for him now. Without his involvement you would not be permitted to purchase these girls". This makes the Doctor look back at me and drop his head.

"Doctor, I need to know the money situation here so I can do my accounting. How much did you pay for these two girls today?" I questioned.

"I paid the normal sir", said the Doctor.

"What is that?" I questioned.

"$200", he answered.

"I am NOT seeing that as the normal, Doctor", I said with authority. The doctor appears to be in fear so I push harder. I say, "I know you are removing the parts for sale. I want to know who are
your clients and what are your prices."

"I don't need to tell you that. That is not part of your business" says the Doc.

"I also need to know what you do with the bodies after you harvest them", I demanded.

"No, you get out of my house", he pushed back.

About that time a man walks out from the other room holding a sawed off shotgun.

"Ah, I knew there would be someone like you!" I said to the man who looked unamused.

I made sure Cam was positioned across the room from me for such an occasion.

"Sir, do you work for me?" I growl.

The man pointed the gun and looked at me. Cam stood and got his attention.

With his attention on Cam, I moved in and was able to disarm the unamused man.

I patted him down for concealed weapons for obvious reasons.

My attention went back to the doctor, "So Doc, I don't think I need to be nice to you anymore".

The doctor stood frozen.

"Doctor, what do you do with the bodies after you are finished?" I commanded.

"I dispose of them through the office as I would any other unknown dead person that dies in the office", he explains.

"Ok, now who do you sell these body parts to?" I grilled him.

The doctor looks away and then back at me. "I don't know them" he pled.

Cam gives me the signal that Doc knows…

So I for warned that the town would need a new Doctor. I said we needed to finish this meeting.

I asked Cam if "the one we spoke with last night was still available?".

Cam said yes.

The fear stricken doctor spoke up, "I call a number and they come. I don't know who they are. I just call them and they come".

"Are they expecting a call from you today?" I interrogate.

"No, I just call and they always come" he pleaded further.

"Where did you find them?" I ask.

"I did not, they came to me in my other office out front." He tried explaining.

"How much do you get for the body parts?" I asked.

"How much do you get for the body parts?" I repeated myself, stepping closer.

He looks at the floor as he speaks, "They give me $500 per package. Each body part if it is kidney, or eye or something else, each has its own package and they know how to transport.
Why are you interrogating me?"

I answered sternly, "There are some thieves in my company and I am looking for them. Don't worry if you do what I ask and give me what I want you will be able to return to your normal business. If you don't, well let's not talk about that."

I give the gun to Cam and ask if he knows how to use it. He does! I tell him to keep watch. I take the nurse into the other room just outside of the others view. I interrogate her and find she is a willing participant. This is common for woman in these countries. They do what they are told and don't complain. So I use this when I talk to her. I try to get

her to tell me how she feels about what she is doing. She won't answer, it is obviously too painful. Instead she explains how she has family and needs to have income.

I strike a deal with her, "I will take care of you if you help me".

She is happy about this but tries not to show it.

She tells me that the girls are asleep in the other room awaiting surgery.

She also tells me they look ill but are merely weak and malnourished.

They could be healed under hospital care.

I step away and think. The next move I make could be a really bad one if all does not go to plan. I take her into the room with the girls. They are under anesthesia. I looked only through my peripheral vision as means to keep my composure.

The door has a bolt lock with a key in it. I remove the key and take it.

I ask her if she will start helping the girls. She agrees. I confirm I will take care of her is she does this. I close the door behind me as I leave her to complete her task.

Cam is still watching the others with hawk eyes. It almost makes me chuckle because I did not see him like this before. I knew he had to have skills with the job he does here but I had yet to see it all.

I ask Cam to keep an eye on the nurse, make sure she is not trying to make a call to turn us in. He does this without delay.

My business is with the Doctor. I pay him cash for the two girls, plus a little extra.
I tell him they are mine now and he will not have to do this work today.

My next order of business is with the "guard". I sit close to him as I thank him for being so quiet and cooperative now. He nods his head yes. I ask him to sit also and he does. The doctor is still sitting and looking down.

"Doctor, what time do you usually call them?" I ask.

"I have called them at all hours." He admits.

"How does it work?" I ask.

"I call and say I have packages, they ask how many, then they tell me how long." He explained

"Then what?" I bark!

"About an hour later they arrive in a van to collect." He said.

"Do they pay you at that time?" I ask.

"Yes", he says.

"Who else is here when they come?" I ask.

"Just the Nurse and I" he confesses.

I have to take a deep breath and collect my thoughts for a moment. I wonder how we will make
this all happen. In this line of work, you learn to improvise as you go. I learned that one mishap can lead to certain death. Time is a commodity I do not currently possess. I have to act fast and think faster.

The longer I stay the more likely I will not survive. Think big or go home.

I came to collect information that would save lives. My attention was on the masses while at the same time on the two who lay dormant before me. This had become my passion. The deeper I step into this the more I think I can do it. So for now I am going with it. Cam is back in the room now and whispers to me that all is good and knows her family. I bring Cam up to speed about the process. We have the doctor dial the number and ask for a pickup of 5 packages. Cam shares the phone with him to make sure that all is said. Now we wait and see if we get killed or not.

I have Cam tell the nurse that she will ride with us and the girls to a hospital. The doctor and his friend here will stay with me until the delivery man arrives. I bring Cam up to speed. When the deliver man arrives we will go with him bringing the nurse and girls. Cam looks at me with wild eyes and agrees. I turn my attention to the doctor and his friend and explain the situation to them. I tell the friend that I just promoted him and after we leave he can go home and have fun for the rest of the week, but he should do it in another town because he cannot speak of this to anyone. If he fails to do this I will not give him his bonus and pay raise and remove him from the organization. Then I give him an evil look. He receives this, smiles and says no problem. I know I got through to him and Cam laughs. I turn to the doctor and ask him if I need to take him with us,

and he says no. I don't trust the doctor but I believe he will do as he is told at least for awhile, but by then I will be gone.

It is about time for the delivery man to arrive. I look out the window. Then I look to Cam and tell him they are in place. Cam a little confused then smiles and asks if it is who he thinks it is. I tell him yes. I look at the doctor and tell him I have someone to make sure he does not talk about this and that he is a good boy. I can tell by the look of the doctor that he takes me seriously. I tell him he can continue his business as usual tomorrow and if he behaves he will never see me again. I also tell him this is a good thing for him. He nods and drops his head again to look at the floor. Just then is a knock at the door and one person enters. Cam steps in behind him and has the shotgun to his back. The guy does not resist and looks like he is going to piss his pants. I let him know this is a different delivery and all would be fine. He would receive his normal fee and a little more. He only needs to take us where he was going. He is either a good actor or really scared. I think he is scared. Cam agrees. Cam gets the nurse and carries one of the girls to the van. The nurse carried the other one and I hold onto the delivery man. I look at the doctor and he looks away. I tell the friend of his to go have fun and he smiles and leaves. We are in the van and look for anything out of place. It is simple and can see it is used for this service. The man is so scared that he can not even drive so Cam takes over. The nurse confirms the girls are fine and makes them as comfortable as she can. The deliveryman explains to Cam where to go find a big hospital in the next city. I am almost confused. We are taken stolen organs to a major hospital.

Miraculously, no catastrophic events occurr along the way. We were able to park right next to the entrance. The

delivery man tells us to go inside and say we have organ deliveries for Dr. John. Then they send a man out with a cart to collect the packages. Then I follow to the desk and get paid. I leave and that is it. We ask if they know him and how do they pay him. He tells us maybe but there are many who do this and they pay in cash. I give him the money he would have made and about half more and can see an ease in his demeanor. So the plan is to all go in with the girls. The nurse will get them treated. What ever they needed, I would pay the bill.

The nurse also tells me she will take them home with her and find homes for them or keep them herself. So we do just that. Our brood enters the lobby. This hospital is not that bad it seems this is one of the more modern in this country. It is a cash only basis and therefore not busy. It must be only the rich that can afford to come here. They take the girls with the nurse into an exam room with a doctor. It is not Dr. John, so now time to snoop.

Over at the nurse's desk was Cam talking and almost flirting, creating diversion. I sit with the delivery man away from the desk. He has calmed down. I assure him when we leave he will also and nothing more about all this will be said. He agrees and I told him he can continue what he does and he will never see me again but I tell him he should find another line of work. I also ask him if he had ever seen this doctor but he had not only the desk people, and the ones that come out for the packages. Cam comes back and says Dr. John does work here and he usually has foreign patients. So it all fits. It is not long after that and our nurse comes out and tells us the girls are going to be fine, they just need a lot of rest and loving. The Doctor's here asked why they had been drugged. She explained she is a nurse; her doctor had an emergency and had to leave. So she brought them here. They were given medicines and IV

fluids. The Doctors wanted them to stay the night for observation but she did not want to leave them.

We eventually all pack it back into the van. The delivery man chauffeurs us to the home of another nurse friend. The delivery man is up to driving now and seems somewhat happy about it. We meet with the nurses. Once we have dropped off the nurse and the girls, the driver is on his way. Cam and I go to a coffee shop to plan.

I can tell that Cam really likes this new job with me. I give him a large some of money to take to the nurse. I inform him to instruct her to leave her work with the doctor. She is now free to move to a safer city. The money would set her up for four years. Even Cam is surprised by the dollar amount.

The wages here can be so sparse. With the money my bosses gave me up front, I was able to move a few mountains like it was nothing. I tell him to find me later and continue this journey.

Now is the time to wrap this up. It could be deemed easy if I were to finish the job, turn in the thief to my bosses, get the rest of my money and go away. I could apply what I have learned in a really useful way and walk away. I chose the more expansive direction. I found resolve in this objective and knowledge. There is no way I can walk out now; I am in too deep in the gamble. Just one more bet in the slots and I will win back all my losses.

I call around to my buddies for Intel that is useful to me for my situation. All of this leaves me with little option. It is looking like I may have to bail out. I sit and stare at the life on the street and inspiration comes to me so I get to work. I call in several favors from my inner circle

A plan is set to go off early the next evening.

I wait patiently for Cam.

We are nearing the finish line and it is time to tighten our belts.

I tell him to go get some rest and talk with his family about making a move anywhere he wants to go. It will need to happen directly after this event tomorrow night. It should be far away from here. He tells me it's done and they are ready. So he heads off and I go back to my place. There I lay down to rest and perfect my plan and exit strategy.

By the time I am awake, I have everything in place to see if any of last nights events leaked out.

I get with Cam and have him make the rounds to see if there is any noise. We meet up later for lunch. Nothing seems to be different. Many of the managers are not well pleased with me snooping around like I have. So it is time to let Cam in on a few things…

I let Cam in on my plan to identify the thief to the partners. I would include the police to assist in the apprehension of the thief. I would make it clear that all would be converging in the casino at 9pm. I identified the thief to Cam. I explained that I would have proof tying him to the theft. My proof included testimony from others incriminating him over the last year. The hoot is they didn't know they were testifying. So there will be no doubt he is the source I was hired to catch. I
Further explained to Cam how important it is for him to be strong until the fireworks end. There will be big fireworks. The conflict he feels over what he has been doing will end

tonight. The sickness may not go away but his part in it will be done and forgiven. I tell him I may call on him again in the future if things go my way but he will always have a choice and I will never leave his wife and kids out of the decision. I grab Cams arm and lead him to the police station. I find the chief and tell him about a big event tonight and that he will need everyone he can get to be at this event. He begins to question me but I fill him full of ego and tell him how important his future depends on how tonight goes.

Chief is putting on the pressure for more information. I tell him it's a serious matter that he will be needed in. I reassure him that everything he wants to know will be revealed in this meeting.
As I leave his desk he is already on the phone instructing others to be in attendance tonight.
I shake his hand, make eye contact, and tell him to be ready. He believes me.

Cam and I walk out and head to the edge of town. Cam is super serious now, wondering what we are doing, but keeping silent as promised. As we get further away from any buildings and are
pretty much alone in the country side. We stop the car and get out. I pour us both a cup of
coffee from an old school thermos I brought. I light up my cigar and offer one to Cam. He declines but accepts the flame for his cigarette instead.

Cam is looking a bit nervous now. He must be wondering if I am going to let him in on what will happen next. I get Cam to look toward the mountain and tell him to smile. He looks confused so I laugh. I tell Cam they need his picture so he does not get killed. Cam looks toward the mountain and I signal the mountain. My friends came as I requested.

They revealed them selves to him by removing camo from all twelve trucks. There they waited patiently to be activated. They covered up again, disappearing back into the landscape. Cam looks at me, then back at them and back at me. He drops his coffee and looks weak in the knees. I console and comfort him, that he is protected and they are our allies. They needed to identify you in order to defend and assist.

He blurts out, "Dog, who are they? What are they?"

So I tell him, "They are my friends. Tonight they will be there when we need them."

He questions further, "Dog, are people going to get killed?"

So I decide to let him in on their role, "Cam, after I tell you, I need you to forget until this is all over. Can you do that?"

"But!" he interrupts.

I attempt to sooth his nerves by reiterating that no one has to die.

"All the little girls that work here in these places you managed, well they are all going to leave tonight and go to places they can be helped and given a place they can be something in life. The sick will have treatment, the hungry will be fed, the ones who need adults to take care of them will have those adults and there will be schooling and most of all love" I said.

Cam cries so I help him sit down.

"Cam you are responsible for this to happen. Without you and spirits guidance I don't think this has a chance. So thank you", I say from the heart.

"Dog….." he laments.

I interrupt to tell him, "Call me Z, that is my real name, but remember to forget that."

With eyes wide open he asks, "Z, who are you?"

"I am your friend and will always be your friend" I say in order to simplify things.

Cam silently looks at me while shaking his head, trying to wrap his mind around this new reality.

"So Cam, are we good?" I ask.

"I think so. Yeah Z. We are good. I am good" he says with a deep sigh of relief.

"Ok, then it is time to forget this until it is over" I request.

We head back to town. I have Cam retrieve the thief with a story, getting him to the casino without suspicion. This is easy to do because they are always having on call meetings. Cam also will have him bring as many as he can with him leaving behind a skeleton crew in all the brothels. As for me, I head to the partners house. I called ahead so both would be there and told them to bring the rest of the money. Jam sounded elated. I head back to the hotel to change and collect my things, I would not be back.

I feed my body to allow time for my mind to digest my thoughts thoroughly.

I have learned to anticipate change so that I can improvise rather than react.

The way I have set it up will not leave much choice but to do as I tell them.

The Police and other V.I.P.'s will be present when this erupts.

My team will slowly emerge into town when they see me taking the partners into the casino.

After I am fed and relaxed I head out on the beginning of the end of this education.

It is a short drive to Nha's house so I take my time. When I arrive, the gates are opened.

It seems now I am an honored guest or walking into my final moments.

I don't take anything lightly. This has almost been too simple.

I accept any gift horses that come my way.

I arrive at the Casino, park a few blocks away, give myself a clean approach and escape route.

I make my way to the Casino where I can see my plan is working. So many of those I want to keep busy have arrived.

If there are loose strings now it is too late but as I can see with all the people here any resistance will be minimal. As I

walk in everyone makes way for me. I get to the back of the Casino in a separate room I find Jam and Nha sitting waiting for me.

"You are both early my friends" I say.

I scan the room, besides my partners there are 4 body guards. I brought with me all the files and notes I collected in the beginning and those that I kept collecting as the days passed. I solved this problem of the missing money in hours after I made the deal with my partners. I had to collect the info as I was learning what I came here for. Any two bit investigator could have solved this easily. The situation is this, the bosses are not self made, but made by circumstances. Then muscle outweighs brain.

"So Dog, what you find?" they demanded.

So I explain, "I find your thief and I have documented it so that you can verify it all.
I have witnesses, dates, times and locations".

"How did you get witnesses?" they questioned further.

"They didn't know they were witnesses. I figured out what was going on. To confirm what I already knew, I asked questions to confirm who, what, when, where, and why of the thief" I answered with pride.

I push the evidence toward them to observe.

I ask one of the body guards to get me coffee with cream. He looks at Jam who nods his head. The guard leaves and as he opens the door I can see many employees gathered outside the door including the Police. I invite the chief in. He happily comes in and I shake his hand. He takes a seat

with my partners. They all talk as they look over the papers and documents. I field questions as they come out and they continue to read and look at the pictures I took. They are so amazed and disturbed that this happened; I can see the anger rise.

"Dog, it is obvious you have found the thief but we can only guess who it is, you do not include this in your report," they questioned.

"Yes, that is correct. I have this and it cannot be disputed. If this was to go to court it would be over in moments. I know this will not be in any court. As both of you are the judge, jury and executioner. There is a matter of money," I remind them.

"Yes, yes, we have it and it is yours. You have done what we ask," Nha says with a smile. He puts a large envelope on the table and I pick it up. I count it and it is all there. I place the package back on the table and show no emotion.

"What is wrong, you want more?" they question me.

Their faces look a bit worried as both wait for me to speak.

The guard comes back in and serves my coffee. I sit down and light a cigar. I check and make sure the door is closed.

"My friends, your trusted manager Cam is bringing him here now. When he arrives we will move into that smaller room over there with no guards. At this time I will make my claim and turn over the rest of the paper trail. Simultaneously, Cam and I will make our exit. I will collect the package and never more be seen." I say.

"My one request is that I am granted enough time to get out of the casino and be on my way," I say.

"Then you can do what you wish with this thief. I do suggest that you approach this slowly and let him talk so that he can dig a bigger hole with other names so you can add these to your list of punishments. I do not claim to know all about what you want in this business. I do not want to tell you what to do... Yet I have learned that with patients you can rid your self of the disease fully rather than just feeling good for a short time until it returns," I say.

"Do you agree to this?" I ask.

"Yes, thank you. We understand and agree." They said. "We would like to see him dead so it is clear you are correct that it is time to be patient. Let us learn more." They said.

I instructed to "Give it an hour or so. When you have everything you need then act!"

They reread the material and grew infuriated.
A knock at the door interrupts the moment.
I open it and the guard escorts in Cam and the unsuspecting thief.
The thief is oblivious as to what this is all about.
I frisk him to be sure he is unarmed.
All clear so I make sure he has no escape.
Cam hands over the rest of the evidence that names him as thief complete with photos.
I pass them around and watch as they turn red with anger and high blood pressure.
The thief is getting nervous now and looks at the door. I grab his arm and bring his focus back to the table of men

who are discovering his guilt. I ask the group if they are satisfied. Void of joy, they nod their head yes.

I gather the package and Cam for our exit. I plant the seed with the guards to pay attention to the doorway because it is about to become loud. As we leave, we quickly pass through the crowd of employees who are waiting. We get to the street and move to my car. I can see Cam is a bit nervous and relieved at the same time. My partners never asked me to return the car so I drive it to the center of the brothel, where I will leave it.

I see our transport trucks in two of the locations. We enter one while our team quickly
extract the girls. They accomplish this with little noise and zero casualties.
Things are how I imagined them, few employees and little attention.

I check in with my team commander via radio with news that all is going according to plan.
All the girls are accounted for and in the trucks. The employees are wrangled and kept in different trucks. They will be moved in an opposite direction to be left in the middle of nowhere as to eliminate any threat.

Cam is looking better now, thinking it is about over. I keep him with me to witness what we are going to do with the kids. We join the caravan of trucks. We will briefly meet at a Buddhist temple where one of my friends has arranged some help for us with monks, nuns, and other good Samaritans that want to help. When I saw this I really could not believe it. You know in this work you find so much avoidance of people actually standing up and helping you begin to act on your own. You cannot depend on anyone and it is hard. So when you see people standing up even

when it could cost them their lives you explode inside. Even though I know why everyone I talk to that walks away or does not want to hear more, I understand. Some people can't handle it or try to dismiss it thinking it is a scam. I can't blame them. At the same time it saddens me because it is our world. Humanity, for many, has become less important than self. Humanity is my passion and I will not stop. Cam is feeling my joy and sees that I am weakened at the sight of so many people helping. He puts his hand on my shoulder and looks me in the eyes and says, Thank You. I hug him and say, no, thank you...

******

Shaking off the burst of emotion inside, I gather myself and meet some of the people. A nun emerges from the crowd and moves directly toward me. I know this could be bad or good, nuns are really tough people and you don't ever want to get on their bad side. She begins to smile as she approaches and I am relieved. She introduces herself and I introduce her to Cam. She tells us the plan they have to get the kids to proper places where they can heal. She tells me I must leave before they realize what happened and look for me. I know this and already have the same plan. I tell her I just need to see this play out right now to remember. She asks me why I decided to do this. I simply said the first thing to came to mind which was, I had to. I guess that was the right answer because she smiled and walked away. When you find your passion you don't behave like you used to. You act more than think. The present moment happens and you look back with out regret. I know many will not understand what I just said but some will. I look around to see my team smiling, laughing and feeling good. This seemed simple for them. I think they were looking for

an excuse to do something good with their talents. I keep
Cam with me. I introduce him to everyone and tell them
our story. I show them all appreciation for helping with this
project. A Priest approaches with the head Monk to assure
me of the destination of the kids.

I witness unity among religions for the benefit of humanity.

We are each our own church, temple or monastery when we
live from the brave heart.

We gravitate toward like minds and similar hearts to
achieve results.

I personally thank each and every helper present.

Cam and I go to check on the children in another room.
They are being told what has just happened and what is
going to happen next. It seems very peaceful yet some are
crying. They don't understand much because they are so
young.

Cam weeps.

I touch his arm and say, "Cam, remember, it is not who you
have been but who you are becoming."

We sit and stare for an hour as people disburse in different
directions.
The mission for me is coming to a close.
I have done all that I can do.

The last group of 5 is about to leave. I ask where they are
going and find it is near where Cam's location to meet his
family and complete their journey. I arrange for them to

take him along. I tell him the news and hand over his money, courtesy of Jam and Nha. He sees this and falls to the ground. I laugh at him and help him up. He can now take his family where ever he wants and start their new life with ease. I call him my brother and we do a guy hug. He walks away without a word and looks back several times as he enters the truck.

A few years later a friend tells me where Cam and his family ended up and started an orphanage. Their orphanage caters to children of all sorts but is a special place for former child slaves. That really makes my heart warm. I seek to save one child at a time and when that has happened it is on to the next child. I really believe in this philosophy of when you save one, you are really saving countless. That has proven itself over and over for me.

I continue this work globally.

This work has changed over time and continues to evolve.

I hope to inspire passion for a renewed humanity, one heart at a time.

# Chapter 10

## Human Trafficking Globally and How to Identify

This rapidly spreading virus has become a concern for the entire international community.

No continent is exempt.

The larger legal system has yet to catch up with the desires of global activism.

Some regions are effected more pervasively, due to the economic and social infrastructure of the troubled area.

The global community fails to comprehend the gritty reality of the human trafficking industry.

Instead, a pop culture representation of young, attractive Eastern European females sold into sexual servitude prevail.

There is a murky world of organized crime and human trafficking. It is a parasitic bond.

The syndicates drain the region of vital human resource as they traffic thousands of females into exploitative service.

This affects society as a whole.

STORIES FROM AROUND THE GLOBE:

RUSSIA

Up to seventy percent of women graduating from University can not find employment because organized crime groups control so much of the economy. As a result, those same educated women, and asset to Russia's continues development, often find them selves misled into forced prostitution. Women are recruited using appealing advertisements in newspapers and magazines.
They promise big money and free housing in jobs such as waitress, nanny and go go dancer in America. Sometimes women are assured that they will meet wealthy men in the city who are eager for marriage. Many victims are provided transportation and travel documents but are quickly stripped of identification once they arrive at their destination. When women realize they have been tricked, they often attempt to escape. Mafia thugs subdue women with violence, narcotics, and isolation. Heroine and methamphetamine have been given to the women to get them hooked and dependant on the gang to feed their habit. The mob have photographed the women and sell them on the internet. They also use the photos to threaten to send to family members if they step out of line. Some photos are sold in private auction for thousands of dollars.

These organizations persist over time.

This dark world has repeatedly proven to be highly dangerous, equally, lucrative, and almost impossible to infiltrate.

There is a story about Aya and Bibi, from Kazakhstan. They were among 12 migrant workers held captive in a supermarket for 10 years. Their children were among them as they were promised work in hopes to support their families. Their passports were confiscated and never returned by the traffickers, who said they needed them to officially register them as workers with authorities. They were beaten and forced to work with out pay by the couple who owned the market. They lifted heavy boxes in and out of the shop everyday. The couple used threats of sexual violence to demand subservience. Aya's mother confirmed that two civic activists rescued them and the others. A short criminal investigation was opened and closed. Prosecutors claimed there was no evidence of crime. They are now facing deportation for residing in Russia illegally.

UKRAINIANS:

In 2001, it was estimated that 400,000 women were trafficked for exploitation, sexual or other. (International Organization for Migration). Human trafficking is then, an ambition, a financial incentive of transnational organized crime, not a mere byproduct. Powerful syndicates exert considerable power over various aspects of national life. They use systematic violence and corruption to facilitate their criminal activities. These organizations have varying capacities to inflict economic, physical, psychological, and societal harm. Ukraine has suffered its share of economic, political and social hardship since the collapse of communism. This has caused a subsequent rise in organized crime as a full time profession.

Ukrainians and Raves

I was contacted to find and rescue a 15 year old girl who had been abducted at a rave. This is one of the easiest

places to obtain under age girls. This is a product they can sell. Product is the word for sex slaves in the industry. The family of the girl contacted me, with vital information from her friend who was with her that night. She had also been kidnapped that night, but managed to escape. With her testimony we had the information needed to find her. It had been 2 weeks since the parents contacted the police and FBI. Nothing. When the friend of the abducted said it was the Ukrainians, this stopped me in my tracks. This group is a huge factor in this world, everyone knows not to mess with their hornet nest. I told the family I did not think there would be anything I could do. Still I decided to try. I parked across the street from the body shop, in L.A.,
said to be involved. I waited around to see what I could see. It was an old chop shop type, from the looks of the outside. They are known for holding the girls in a house for the purpose of continuous sex sales. They are also sold online in auctions to the highest bidding individual.
I saw exactly what the friend told me I would see, five men and which cars they drove. At best, I thought I could make a call to police and they would have to check it out.

Not long after, I saw 4 men leave, presumed on lunch break. If I were to have a window of opportunity present itself, here it was. I walked over and planned to act as a customer. I noticed the door was slightly ajar. I noticed a few other workers down a hall, also on lunch break. I creapt through the door and looked around. I found the girl hog tied and gagged on the floor. I felt someone to my right and struck him out. I grabbed the girl and took her to my car. I threw her over my shoulder, got her into the backseat and we sped off. I ungagged her and she screamed and screamed. I explained who sent me. After I felt a safe distance, that no one was following us, I untied her. She bear hugged me. I told her it was not over until I got her home.

There in my backseat she went silent as I drove on into the night toward her parents home. Eventually she fell asleep. She was exhausted and safe. Words can not describe how this all made me feel. Deep gratitude activated. I did not wake her when I pulled into her driveway.
Her father met us at the car and carried her in. Mother in tow the entire way. I made my quiet exit. My job had concluded. This was now family time.

It did not take long to hear through the grape vine that I was being hunted.

I am well aware of how this all works and how to resolve it. I must go find the Boss of this organization at his public place of work. I must find him and talk to him before he finds me.
So I went. It was about saving face. I honored him by offering my services to him. In return he would honor me by releasing me. It was agreed. I was to then stay far away from his businesses and I would live. Done and done.

AFRICA:

I know of many great souls who are combating Human slavery and trafficking here. I have chosen not to fight this war because I do not believe I can make a difference there. I seek to change the world and leave examples of this for people to see what can be done. In Africa it must be started again and again new. This is because of constant change in leaders and government. So in short I cannot make effective change there but by continuing the path I have started there could be change there some day.

My campaign will also NOT include (with few exceptions): The nations of the USA, China, Canada, Russia and UK.

These hold different reasons than Africa.

They have laws and methods that prevent the stopping of this sin.

In the Industrialized countries I would be treated as one of the criminals.

That would end this quest.

SOUTH AMERICA:

I will keep most of the details out of this but enough will be kept in to give you more understanding of how all this works, and why I have chosen the path that I have. My commander was x- military and high up in rank. Very well respected, he would often be chosen for some very high end jobs. This job we would go into now had already had other companies come in and fail.

It pertained to an important group of men from a country needed for business and the economy of the country. This group of important men had a compound that was very well guarded in a South American country. They were kidnapping and buying very young children to be brought to them for religious ceremonies where the child would die in the process. It was mainly sexual if you can call it that. These important men were connected to friends of the government we were hired by. But they had taken kids from other important people so a solution had to be created for everyone to save face. Crazy right!

This job as you can guess drove me to the brink of insanity and calloused my emotions to the point I should not have recovered. Somehow, spirit did. So I can keep doing what I do. The reason other groups before us failed was because this was a very secure compound. We were really good at what we did and that is why I am able to be here to tell you this story. We eventually succeeded in our mission and

ended this evil practice. Yes it was just one of I am sure many but we did what we were hired to do. This is not where it ended.

Once we completed we knew we were not meant to escape. We had too much knowledge of the people involved on both sides so we were prepared. The best military had come after us to remove us. We lost some and because we knew they would come they lost all and because we knew what was coming we were prepared when we won so we could continue our business. It is kind of like playing chess. We had checkmate. If word got out that this government had hired the removal of this group of men it would be disastrous for the world especially that government and that government was in what you call a rock and a hard place. If they did nothing; disaster. If they did something; disaster. That is why we were hired. They had the plan of removing us, but it did not work out that way. Still they won because we let them. Sometimes to win, everyone loses. That is what happened here.

**U.S.A.**

Mauri was 16 when she was prostituted on the streets of Honolulu. She was a normal school girl that started to hang out with the vermin in her school. She liked the bad boy and tough girl sort of thing. Not unlike many teenagers rebelling against authority and parents. He boyfriend got her into drugs and sex then sharing her with his friends and so on. Mauri started to think about all this. But the drugs and parties kept her going deeper into this sort of life. It escalated when her boyfriend pimped her out and kept the money. There was no escape. her pimp threatened to kill her family if she did not go out and work the streets each night. Mauri was beaten for buying food with the money she earned. Mauri finally escaped and was picked up by

law enforcement. She is now in a rehabilitation program and has reunited with her parents. Her road to recovery has been long and difficult. She suffers from terrible flashbacks and severe depression, and has even attempted suicide. Mauri says she was lucky to get out alive, "The longer you stay the less hope you have."

Another true story is about 32 men with intellectual disabilities and a foul turkey farm. The men were held as "employees" for 20 years in horrid conditions. The company "housed" the men in so called "bunk houses". They endured filthy conditions such as decrepit mattresses, bug infestations, lack of heating, and a leaking roof. The men were abused both verbally and physically. They earned .40 cents an hour. They were denied access to health care. They were forced to carry heavy weights as punishment. One case was reported of being handcuffed to his bed. A law suit was filed under the Americans with Disabilities Act. A jury awarded the men approximately $3,000,000. The largest sum in verdict history for the U.S. Equal Employment Opportunity Commission.

MEXICO:

In many of the poorer countries there are ads in newspapers and flyers posted for house cleaners and child care nannies. They target the younger and desperate females hoping for a way to support their families. This is a similar story of Lily; a young girl from El Salvador. Lilly was unemployed and unable to find a job. She decided to leave in search.of work. A family friend promised to take Lilly to the United States, but instead took her to Mexico. When Lilly discovered that she had been tricked, she ran away and ended up in an area where other migrants like herself waited to go to back home. One day a group of men invited her and the others to join their organization, the Zetas, a notorious drug cartel.

They said they would give her work and feed her. When she joined them, she was forced into prostitution, tricked for the second time. Lilly was drugged the first day and woke up with a "Z" tattoo, branded for life. She was forced to ingest drugs and was never allowed to travel unaccompanied. After three months, her aunt in El Salvador paid for her freedom and she was finally freed. Her traffickers were brought to court but were acquitted. Lilly will not testify again.

THAILAND:

Kyila and Mia, both 16 years old, were promised work as domestic helpers in Thailand. With the help of five different local brokers, they traveled from Burma walking all day and night through a forest, crossing a river in a small boat, and spending a few nights in various homes along the way. In this process they have to surrender their passports and documentation. This is because it will be given to the person who buys them for whatever purpose they choose to use them for. They also often sell the documentation. Once they arrived, they were placed in a meat-processing factory and forced to work from 4 a.m. to 11 p.m. Kyila and Mia complained to the factory manager of the hard work and long working hours, and told him this was not what they were told they would be doing in Thailand. The factory manager told the girls they owed him for their "traveling expenses" from Burma to Thailand and could not leave until it was paid off. He continued to subtract their "debt" from what little income they received. Eventually the girls found a way to contact one of their relatives in Burma who then contacted an NGO; the organization arranged their safe removal from the factory. They were lucky because normally the business owner is working with key government officials that are also in on

it. Slavery is big business that brings in big money. This economy then fills the pockets of greedy politicians. They are now in a Thai government shelter in Bangkok, receiving counseling while waiting for repatriation.

Tala was a seven year old when she was lured away from her parents by a couple who owned the field where her family worked. While enslaved, she was forced to take care of cats and dogs for the couple's pet grooming shop. For five years, Tala's parents hoped to see her again, never knowing how she disappeared or where she might be. They never imagined that Tala was close, enduring torture and abuse. If Tala did not do her job properly, she was kicked, slapped, and beaten with a broom. Sometimes the couple locked her in a cage and poured boiling hot water over her. On one occasion, the traffickers cut off her ear lobe with a pair of scissors. One day, she climbed a concrete fence of the house while chasing a cat and realized she was free. A neighbor called the police and she was taken to a nearby shelter where her mother identified her. The couple was arrested and charged with various charges, including torture, detainment against will, enslavement, and kidnapping. The couple posted bail and escaped. This is also normal in these countries. As for Tala, injuries on her arms affected her muscles, she can no longer move her left arm. For now, she is safe with her family and is beginning her mental, emotional, and physical journey to recovery.

PHILIPPINES:

A young lady named Dalisae signed a contract with an employment agency in the Philippines to work as a housemaid in Qatar for $400 a month, plus room and board. But when she arrived, her employer said he would pay her

only $250 a month. This is a common ploy of employers in this country. She knew her family back in the Philippines depended on her earnings and felt she had no choice but to stay to help her family. She quickly realized that her low pay was not the only unexpected condition of her work situation. She was fed one meal a day, leftovers from the family's lunch: "If no leftovers, I didn't eat." She worked seven days a week. When she was finished working in her employers' house, she was forced to clean his mother-in-law's house, and then his sister's without any additional pay. After eight months, Dalisae tried to leave but her boss just laughed and said "You can't quit." As a domestic worker not covered under the labor law, Dalisae was subject only to the restrictive kafala. This is a sponsorship system; meaning that she could not resign without her employer's permission. She could not change jobs, leave the country, get a driver's license, or open a checking account without the permission of her employer. She also learned that her employer could withdraw sponsorship at any time and send her back home. She fled and joined 56 other women who sought shelter at the Philippines Overseas Labor Office.

**CHINA:**

One specific Asian gang is referred to as the "Triads." The group has been very successful in the United States creating cells in New York, Miami, San Francisco, Los Angeles, Chicago, Boston, and Houston. Human trafficking has become the crime of choice not only because it is safer than offenses such as drug trafficking, but because there is low overhead. Century old cargo carriers are used for travel and occupancy is triple what it should be resulting in rancid conditions onboard vessels. Traffickers may charge as much as $35,000 per immigrant but only require a $100 deposit. Once the person arrives in the United States they

are obligated to pay the remainder of their debt or become enslaved by the Triads either in sweatshops or prostitution houses. Gang members threaten death or violence against them or their families if they attempt escape.

The Triad home base is believed to be in Hong Kong. They also have heavy control of Taiwan where billions in profit flow through legitimate businesses. In Spain, the Triad gangs have infiltrated a small Chinese community and have corrupted both law enforcement and government agencies. When someone dies in this town, the Triad gangs simply give the person a new identity by recycling their legal citizenship documents. Nobody ever questions why the population is skewed and there are no deaths year after year. Triad groups are masters in exploiting foreign government and often pay large sums to agencies masked as donations to the military or economic development when the money is actually bribe money for access to ports and facilities needed for their operations. There are many hierarchical groups within Asian organized crime.It is decentralized making it difficult to obtain information regarding international connections once an arrest is made.

In addition, there are other large organized crime gangs. The Big Circles is a loose alliance of criminal gangs founded by former Red Guards of the Cultural Revolution. Their individual names refer to the detention centers where they were "re-educated." They are active in snakehead human trafficking and other criminal operations.


KENYA:

There are many ways to attract younger people and gain their trust. One way is through schools and the need for money to pay his tuition. So it is not just one country but

many countries and with just small adjustments the ability to lure kids into a situation they cannot get out of is rather easy like in this story. Latu was desperate to find a job to pay for his university school tuition. While in town one day, Latu met a man who said he needed people to work for him at a factory in Kenya. Hoping this job would help pay for his tuition, Latu agreed to accompany the man to Kenya and met with him the very next day to travel. Other men and women also met them to travel to Kenya. Eventually they arrived at their final destination in Kenya at a huge house. The man, who had earlier been kind to them all, suddenly became rude and ordered them to give him their identification and phones. They were shown a video of a man who had been suffocated with a bag because he attempted to escape. They were all told that they would not be working at a factory, but rather would be working as sex slaves. Every room had a camera and they were recorded while they were forced to have sex with strangers. After a month and half of captivity, Latu was allowed to accompany his captors into town. When they stopped to have lunch, he ran away. Law enforcement officials in Kenya opened an investigation and Latu was able to return to Uganda and received medical attention. In this case he was lucky because in these places the local government and police change policies as often as a daily basis at times.

SOUTH AFRICA:

A man at a local coffee shop that had a lot of foot traffic from younger people was passing out flyers offering work. This always attracts a lot of attention due to poor economic conditions. Chew talked to this man and was offered a better life in South Africa working for an organization that

ran a Boy Scouts group. Excited about the job, he left Zimbabwe for South Africa. Instead of receiving the job he was promised, he was forced to work every day on a farm for a piece of bread and some water. For six months, Chew was transported between farms in Zambia and South Africa, enduring physical and other abuses, dreaming of the day he would escape. When Chew and a friend finally did escape, they made their way to Cape Town, a security guard on the street noticed them and when they told their story to him he helped them to safety. Through the Department of Social Development, they were taken to an NGO, which helped provide support and services to them both. Chew suffers from post-traumatic stress, but decided to stay in South Africa, hopeful that he will still find that better life that led him away from home.


EGYPT:

In many places of extreme poverty, females are thought of as a burden to a family. They are often sold to most anyone who wants to buy them. This way the family has money and no longer has to support the girl. Susan was only 10 when her father sold her to an Egyptian family to serve as a domestic worker. Despite her protests, Susan accompanied the family back to Egypt. Once there, she was forced to work excessive hours, never received compensation, and her passport was confiscated. She was locked in the house where she was physically and emotionally abused daily. During her six years of enslavement, she was not allowed to speak to her family, when her relatives tried to reach her by phone, Susan's employer would hang up the phone. One day, she summoned the courage to escape. She was arrested shortly after her escape for immigration violations, but with the cooperation of an international NGO and Egyptian authorities, she was released from detention and recognized

as a trafficking victim. While staying at a government shelter in Egypt, the international NGO arranged for Susan's return to her country in West Africa. Once there, UNICEF and the child protection police arranged for her to stay in a designated shelter for trafficking victims while her family was located. After three weeks, she was reunited with her family and given the chance to enroll in vocational training as part of her reintegration process. Susan looks to brighter days now and hopes to open an Egyptian restaurant in her town. The sad thing is that many times the family will take her back only to sell her again. We hope this will not happen this time.

FRANCE:

Many times parents will die in these poor countries and the oldest sibling will take the responsibility to care for the younger ones. Ogo was on such lady. Since her parents passed away, Ogo had been struggling to care for her younger brothers. An acquaintance offered to take her abroad and find her a job. Ogo was ecstatic; she accepted his offer, believing that she would now be able to help her family in Nigeria. Before setting off to Europe, she was taken to a juju priest to seal the deal with local magic. During the ceremony, she vowed she would obey her boss in Europe and pay back her travel expenses. The "spell" called for death if she failed to fulfill her oath. It was not too long before she realized that something was wrong, she had joined about 30 other women in an open-back truck headed toward the Sahara Desert. They finally reached their destination and were met by a "madam" in France who told her she owed travel expenses for her passage to Europe and would be forced to pay it back by selling her body. She worked the streets as many as 20 hours a day and was forced to pay for her own food and clothes as well as for rent that would be deducted from her earnings. In almost all

of these cases they will never pay off their debt. Despite the juju oath, she was encouraged by a man she befriended to go to the police. Once at the police station, she explained her situation. Her traffickers were arrested but so was she, for being in France illegally. Before her deportation, workers at the detention center gave her money out of good will for her safe return to Nigeria. She is now building her life again and says, "I am very much stronger than juju."

INDIA:

It is common for placement agencies to sell applicants information to people who are looking for a slave that is young just like in this case. Naven was 14 years old when a placement agency found him a job as a domestic worker for a couple with two children. For the two years he served the family, Naven was confined to the house, never allowed to leave. He was beaten regularly for trivial matters and, on several occasions, branded with hot tongs. Unable to endure his situation anymore, he escaped. He ran to the police station and was helped. Naven is living in a children's home and receiving counseling. The couple have been charged and are out on bail awaiting a court date but that is unlikely to happen.

\*\*\*\*\*\*

ADDITIONAL INFORMATION ON IDENTIFICATION

**Use of Social Media in Schools**

Schools provide the perfect opportunity for traffickers because they are populated with vulnerable victims

especially with the increase in digital on school campuses, traffickers are finding that it is much easier to facilitate their crimes through a simple text message. Just ask yourself how many 12-17 year olds possess cell phones. Approximately 93% of 12-17 years olds go online, and 63% of them do so every day. Fifty-four percent of teens have also received unwanted texts or spam and 15% have received sexually suggestive text messages, including nudes. The availability of mobile technology that children and teenagers have access to makes them especially vulnerable to a trafficking operation, with school campus the most likely place. In an effort to prevent human trafficking through the use of digital technology, school personnel should implement policies that prohibit children and teenagers from using their cell phones on school grounds, with the exception of emergencies.

**Recognizing the Signs of Trafficking**

Traffickers can play the quintessential role of a parent, student, or friend. Trafficking victims range in ages from three to eighteen years old and have been found to be predominantly females for sexual exploitation. Males are also trafficked for sexual exploitation; however, evidence shows that they are more likely to be used for forced labor. Both traffickers and trafficking victims can be found in schools, playgrounds, and other places where children and teenagers congregate as well as in larger places such as, inner-cities, suburbs, parties, malls and rural areas.

**Academic Behavioral Physical Emotional Social**

Here is a list of the most common signs:.
Academically unengaged
Avoids eye contact visible bruises and scars
Low self-esteem

Has much older partners
Performs under grade level
Gaps in memory
Appears malnourished
Exhibits depression
Anxiety or fear
Lives in an unstable or abusive home
Sudden change in academic performance
Resists being touched
Shows signs of drug or alcohol addiction
Exhibits sudden outburst of anger
Has a sexual online profile
Appearance of physical and sexual abuse
Scripted and or rehearsed answers to casual questions
He or she appears very young and fearful and overly
submissive
An older male at a hotel with a younger female whom she
calls "daddy."
Look for tattoos of man's name or slang name
Someone not allowed going into public alone or speaking
for themselves.
Is fearful, anxious, depressed, submissive, tense, or nervous
and or paranoid
Fearful or anxious about topic of law enforcement
Person is "just visiting" and won't tell anyone a permanent
address
Person is unsure where they are or able to say where they
have been recently
You see a young person at a truck stop. Children generally
don't go to truck stops

**Visible Indicators of Human Trafficking may Include:**

Heavy security; IE barred windows, pad locked doors,
isolated location, electronic surveillance.

Women are never seen leaving the premises unless escorted.

Victims live on the same premises as the brothel or work site. For labor trafficking, victims are often prohibited from leaving the work site, which may look like a guarded compound from the outside.

Victims are kept under surveillance when taken to a doctor, hospital or clinic for treatment. Trafficker may act as a translator.

Constant stream of foot traffic from men coming and going.

Trafficking victims are kept in bondage through a combination of fear, intimidation, abuse, and psychological control. While each victim will have a different experience, they share common threads that may signify a life of indentured servitude.

Trafficking victims live a life marked by abuse, betrayal of their basic human rights, and control under their trafficker. The following indicators in and of themselves may not be enough to meet the legal standard for trafficking, but they indicate that a victim is controlled by someone else and the situation should be further investigated.

## What Is the Profile of a Human Trafficking Victim?

Most trafficking victims will not readily volunteer information about their status because of fear and abuse they've suffered at the hands of their trafficker. They may also be reluctant to come forward with information from despair, discouragement, and a sense that there are no viable options to escape their situation. Even if pressed,

they may not identify themselves as someone held in bondage for fear of retribution to themselves or family members. However, there are indicators that often point to a person held in a slavery condition. The health characteristics of a trafficked person. Trafficked individuals may be treated as disposable possessions without much attention given to their mental or physical health.

Health problems evident in a victim may include:

Malnutrition and/or dehydration
Poor personal hygiene
Sexually transmitted diseases
Signs of rape or sexual abuse
Bruising and/or broken bones
Signs of untreated medical problems
Critical illnesses including diabetes, cancer or heart disease
Post-traumatic stress or psychological disorders


**Red flags for police or aid workers during an intake:**

Does not hold his/her own identity or travel documents

Suffers from verbal or psychological abuse, feels intimidated, degraded and frightened

Has another person controls all the money, having little or no pocket money themselves

Is extremely nervous around their "translator" (who may be their trafficker)

If the individual is a foreigner, unable to speak the language in the country where they reside or work.

**The phases of human trafficking:**

1. The process of human trafficking begins with the recruitment or abduction of a person.
2. Then the transportation from place of origin to place of destination; often another country.
3. Next, the exploitation phase; the victim is forced into sexual/labor servitude.
4. Finally, Profit Laundering. This last phase does not involve the victim.

Thus further links to other criminal offences such as:
Weapons
Drugs
Migrant smuggling

These phases narrow down to:
a. Recruitment
b. Transportation
c. Exploitation
d. Profit Laundering

## CONCLUSION
## HAIKU


**An extreme warning
We all must now do something
Children are enslaved.**

# The Quest

The Vision

The Quest envisions the most vulnerable people to transform economically, socially, and spiritually. To show the world who, what, where, when, and how to make a difference in different environments. To end poverty and human trafficking around the world.

Our Values

We will serve those who are suffering from poverty and injustice, regardless of color, belief, or gender, as part of plan to redeem, reconcile, and restore the world. We seek to be spiritually humble, and provide relief to lives individually and corporately and how to end poverty.

The Local Community

Our mission brings reconciliation and restoration to others and the environment. The People whether staff, volunteers, clients, beneficiaries, donors, and partners, as important factors in bringing peace, love, and justice. The Quest is a multicultural organization that seeks to understand and respect the multiplicity of cultures among us. As we seek change in the world, we recognize that we, too, are changed, by those we serve in ending slavery.

The Partnerships

Seeking, facilitating, and promoting collaboration among all stakeholders, including local governments, the mission agencies, and the business community. Recognizing partnership as essential to serving the most vulnerable. We believe each expression of The Quest has a unique and independent role in bringing peace and justice to the world and for solutions to poverty.

The Improvements

In all our programs are initiatives and support services. We follow the best practices and standards in a manner that is sustainable to the community from a spiritual, social, and economic perspective. We also seek to apply our human, financial, and products resource in such ways that maximizes impact and sustain benefits to the greatest number of people.

The Empowerment

By prioritizing the leadership and participation of those we serve, whether people, churches, or local institutions, as critical to creating and sustaining change. We seek to catalyze a movement of worldwide volunteers to multiply impact, and we value capacity-building as a means towards that end.

www.thehumanquest999.com

# About the Author

Founder of The Quest.
Zaysan lives in servitude to global humanity.
He has been shot, stabbed, jailed, and left for dead.
Standing up for those who can not stand for themselves.


Facebook : The Quest

Twitter: Zaysan@questslavery

Youtube: The Quest Human Trafficking

The Quest: thehumanquest999.com

About the Editor

J. N. D. is an artist from the beach.
This is her first 120 page edit.
She intended for this book to be read aloud in groups
(Ch1-9).
Listen to her audio reading on youtube.

www.ingramcontent.com/pod-product-compliance
Lightning Source LLC
Chambersburg PA
CBHW030435290526
45786CB00001B/292